Cambridge Elements

Elements in the Philosophy of Mathematics
edited by
Penelope Rush
University of Tasmania
Stewart Shapiro
The Ohio State University

MATHEMATICAL NOTATIONS

Dirk Schlimm
McGill University

Shaftesbury Road, Cambridge CB2 8EA, United Kingdom

One Liberty Plaza, 20th Floor, New York, NY 10006, USA

477 Williamstown Road, Port Melbourne, VIC 3207, Australia

314–321, 3rd Floor, Plot 3, Splendor Forum, Jasola District Centre, New Delhi – 110025, India

103 Penang Road, #05–06/07, Visioncrest Commercial, Singapore 238467

Cambridge University Press is part of Cambridge University Press & Assessment, a department of the University of Cambridge.

We share the University's mission to contribute to society through the pursuit of education, learning and research at the highest international levels of excellence.

www.cambridge.org
Information on this title: www.cambridge.org/9781009472111

DOI: 10.1017/9781009472128

When citing this work, please include a reference to the DOI 10.1017/9781009472128

First published 2024

A catalogue record for this publication is available from the British Library

ISBN 978-1-009-47211-1 Hardback
ISBN 978-1-009-47214-2 Paperback
ISSN 2399-2883 (online)
ISSN 2514-3808 (print)

Mathematical Notations

Elements in the Philosophy of Mathematics

DOI: 10.1017/9781009472128
First published online: December 2024

Dirk Schlimm
McGill University

Author for correspondence: Dirk Schlimm, dirk.schlimm@mcgill.ca

Abstract: This Element lays the foundation for the systematic study of mathematical notations, by both setting a framework, and laying down a program for this study. It is written for everyone who is curious about the world of symbols that surrounds us, in particular researchers and students in philosophy, history, cognitive science, and mathematics education. The main characteristics of mathematical notations are introduced and discussed in relation to the intended subject matter, the language in which the notations are verbalized, the cognitive resources needed for learning and understanding them, the tasks that they are used for, their material basis, and the historical context in which they are situated. Specific criteria for the design and assessment of notations are discussed, as well as ontological, epistemological, and methodological questions that arise from the study of mathematical notations and of their use in mathematical practice.

Keywords: notations, mathematical thinking, external representations, mathematical practice, mathematical methodology

ISBNs: 9781009472111 (HB) 9781009472142 (PB) 9781009472128 (OC)
ISSNs: 2399-2883 (online), 2514-3808 (print)

Contents

1 Introduction

1.1 Toward a Philosophy of Mathematical Notations

Mathematical notations are everywhere. Some symbols, such as '0' and '∞',[1] have an almost mythical allure, and people often enjoy learning about some unsuspected feature of a notation (for example, that combining two 'V's, representing five in Roman numerals, one of them written upside-down, produces the Roman numeral for ten: V + Λ = X).

When using a familiar notation, we are often not aware of the notation at all; rather we *see through it*, almost immediately grasping its meaning. In fact, many people are spontaneously inclined to say that '3' is the *number* three, instead of the Indo-Arabic *numeral* that represents that number. In her famous discussion of the difference between good and bad typography, Beatrice Warde introduced the analogy of drinking wine from a crystal goblet and from a golden goblet: in the first case, we experience the wine without being distracted by the vessel, in the second case, the vessel diverts our attention from the wine. For Warde, good typography is like a crystal goblet.[2]

While parts of the analogy with a crystal goblet also work for good notations, there is one important disanalogy, namely, the presence and nature of the wine. A common misconception about notations, or writing systems in general for that matter, is that they are entirely *derivative* upon previously given content. Accordingly, one might hear the following story: At some point in history people began to refer to *numbers* to express the cardinality of collections of things and employed them for counting the objects in question. Then, in order to facilitate these operations and to record the results, systems of *numerals* were introduced. In this way different notations emerged, which may differ in their pragmatic consequences, but which essentially relate to the same content or subject matter, namely numbers. Although there is some truth to this story, namely that notations can be *motivated* by some understanding of a given subject matter, the derivative view of notations is not general enough to apply to all uses of mathematical notations, perhaps not even to most of the really interesting ones. Too little credit is given to notations under the derivative view.[3]

A second misconception about mathematical notations can arise from assuming too close a connection between a notation and its intended subject matter. Because conceptual innovations often go hand in hand with new notations, the

[1] Double quotation marks in this Element are used for quotations of text, and single quotation marks are used to mention expressions.

[2] Warde (1955).

[3] For more discussion of the derivative view, see Tolchinsky (2003, xvii and 98).

history of mathematics can be told as a progression of increasingly sophisticated mathematical notations. However, this runs the risk of portraying the conceptual changes purely as notational changes, in other words, of giving too much credit to the notations. For example, the current use of algebraic methods in geometry, initiated mainly by Vieta and Descartes, is sometimes presented as an example of a revolutionary change of notation. However, what really lies at the heart of this revolution is a novel mapping between two different subject matters, namely, geometry and algebra, each with its own notations. What is indicated by $y = mx + b$ is a geometric *line* only in an *indirect* sense. Directly, the equation represents a set of pairs of real *numbers* $\langle x, y \rangle$, which are mapped to geometric *points* by means of a system of coordinates.[4] Thus, by heeding a clear distinction between those aspects that depend on the notation and those that depend on the subject matter, a clearer understanding of developments in mathematics can be achieved.

Finally, a third misconception about notations is that one might be inclined to think that they always evolve teleologically, toward the better and more efficient. This view is somewhat comforting because it implies that we are currently using the best tools available, but studies of the development of technology should give us some pause. In fact, advances in technology are not always toward the better and more efficient: otherwise, I would not type this text using a keyboard with a QWERTY layout, which was motivated historically by certain limitations of the mechanics of typewriters; it has persisted until today due to its early adoption also for computer keyboards, despite the fact that more efficient layouts for reducing finger movements have been proposed.

Regardless of their ubiquity, notations have not attracted the attention of many philosophers of mathematics. Presumably, this is because they are interested in an abstract conception of mathematics that is independent of its representations. After all, the fact that five plus seven equals twelve seems to be independent of whether it is written as '$5+7 = 12$' or in Roman numerals as '$\mathrm{V}+\mathrm{VII} = \mathrm{XII}$'. Now, to talk about mathematical objects we need *some* way of representing them, but which way we choose is irrelevant, or so the argument goes. This attitude, however, ignores three crucial contributions of notations to mathematics. First, to formulate any claims, to express any truths, and to arrive at most of these truths, some kind of representation is necessary. These are not merely names for denoting mathematical objects, but *handles*, which allow us to gain insights into the objects they denote by studying their structure and by manipulating them. Second, we actually often *think* in notations rather than in terms of abstract mathematical objects (even when we do *mental arithmetic*,

[4] Historically, this development was much more involved; see, for example, Bos (2001).

most often we manipulate numerals in our mind, rather than numbers). Third, notations can *open up* or *preclude* conceptual possibilities, thus considerably influencing the course of mathematical research.

Getting clearer about the *roles* notations can play in mathematical thought, as mediators between the concrete and the abstract, and about *how* they play these roles, are two of the main aims of a *philosophy of notations*. Indeed, "the illustration of principles which underlie all algebraic notation" was one of the aims explicitly formulated by Peirce (1885) in his paper "On the algebra of logic: A contribution to the philosophy of notation," in which he coined the phrase "philosophy of notation." An important step toward achieving these aims is, of course, to clarify what notations are in the first place. To this, we turn next.

1.2 The Nature of Mathematical Notations

1.2.1 Modalities

We shall restrict our subsequent discussion of mathematical notations to *written* notations that are perceived *visually*. The main reasons for this are that most mathematical notations are of this form and that it streamlines the presentation. We must not forget, however, that other modalities are possible and have indeed been used. The Oksapmin people in Papua New Guinea, for example, represent numerical quantities by pointing at specific parts of their bodies,[5] and the practice of finger counting is widespread across the world. In addition to these *embodied* representations, there are also *auditory* and *tactile* ones, such as number words and the Nemeth Braille Code. While we leave aside the specifics of such notations in this Element, many observations and remarks about written notations do also apply to other modalities, and we certainly consider the study of the latter an important and worthwhile extension of the current project.

1.2.2 Varieties of Notations

To this day, the two-volume work *A History of Mathematical Notations* by Cajori (1928a; 1929) provides the most extensive collection of symbols and notations used throughout the history of mathematics. What is truly remarkable about this work is the diversity of notations that have been employed. For example, Cajori reports "twenty-seven or more varieties of symbols for the calculus of radicals" in use at the end of the sixteenth century, "about thirty-four different notations" for decimal fractions, "at least half a dozen rivals" to denote equality, and "thirty-five different varieties of notation for partial

[5] Saxe (1981).

derivatives."[6] Moreover, different notations for the same mathematical concept can be found even within the writings of a single author. For example, for the relations *greater than* and *less than*, Leibniz used

Γ and ˥, ⚌ and ⚍, > and <, and ⊐ and ⊏

in different publications.[7] International efforts to unify mathematical notations were undertaken by mathematicians in 1895, 1903, and 1908, but they were considered unsuccessful, and in 1924 Cajori concluded: "The primitive source of failure seemed to be the attempt on the part of each individual to secure a *perfect notation*, which was, of course, the one he himself proposed, rather than to *reach an agreement* on a notation."[8] A century later the situation seems to have somewhat changed, through the internationalization of research and publication venues, and the free availability and widespread use of the typesetting software LaTeX. Further research is needed, however, to determine exactly what has changed and what were the driving forces behind this development.

1.2.3 Mathematical Notations

Let us now introduce some definitions of the main notions in the philosophy of notations and their terminology. Simply put:

- A *notational system* is a set of *systematically constructed expressions*.
- Expressions, in turn, are *arrangements* of *characters*.

For brevity we shall also use *notation* in place of 'notational system' and refer to characters and arrangements as *notational elements*. Since we are considering only written notations here, the arrangement can be a linear concatenation, a specific spatial relation (above, below, to the left, to the right, enclosed in, etc.), or any form of juxtaposition, as will be discussed in more detail in Section 2. To get a sense of the ways in which characters can be arranged, the reader is invited to carefully study the following, rather simple examples – note that the point is not to understand what they mean, but to appreciate the variety of possible spatial arrangements:

---

[6] Cajori (1928b, 932–934).

[7] Cajori (1925, 422). To reproduce the wealth of symbols used by Leibniz, the *Philiumm* project, which aims at making accessible a number of Leibniz's unpublished manuscripts, has proposed to add 228 new characters to the Universal Character Set as defined by the Unicode Consortium (https://eman-archives.org/philiumm/node/125, retrieved June 30, 2024). Thanks to David Rabouin for this reference.

[8] Cajori (1928b, 935).

$$\frac{1}{2} \times 3^{(4+5)} \qquad \prod_{i=1}^{n} u_i(x) \qquad \begin{array}{ccc} A & \xrightarrow{f} & B \\ & {\scriptstyle g\circ f} \searrow & \downarrow {\scriptstyle g} \\ & & C \end{array} \qquad \boxed{\begin{array}{c} A \quad B \\ \boxed{B\, \boxed{C}} \end{array}}$$

What makes a notational system *operative* is the presence of rules for manipulating expressions, namely, for transforming one or more expressions into another.[9] Such rules are essential for gaining insights about the subject matter through manipulations of expressions, which is characteristic for mathematical practice. Not all notational systems that occur in mathematics are operative, and operative notations are also used outside of mathematics (e.g., in chemistry and physics). But because mathematics is the paradigmatic domain of such notations, we shall call operative notational systems simply *mathematical notations*.

1.2.4 Notations as Representations and as Languages

The relation between a notation and its subject matter can be conceptualized in different ways, which leads to different intuitions about what notations do and how they work. Some notational systems, for example for music or dance, are designed to represent a given subject matter in such a way that the original source can be recreated more or less faithfully. For such *representational systems*, which are the starting point of Goodman's analysis of notations (discussed in Section 3.1.2), the semantic relation is at the forefront; in Palmer's terms, this is a relation between aspects of a "represented world" and aspects of a "representing world," both of which are functionally independent and of which the represented world is taken to be given independently of the representation.[10]

For notations that are intended to represent an *abstract* subject matter, the representational view is insofar problematic as it is often not clear how that subject matter can be given and accessed independently of a notation in the first place. Moreover, from the perspective of mathematical practice, there are clear cases where mathematicians themselves did not consider their own notations to be fully representational. For example, for Cauchy, "the sign $\sqrt{-1}$ is nothing more than a tool, a calculating instrument" and expressions containing it "taken literally and interpreted according to generally established conventions, do not signify anything and have no meaning."[11] Geometric diagrams that feature in proofs by contradiction, such as in Proposition 6 of Book I of Euclid's *Elements*,

9 See Krämer (2003).

10 Palmer (1978, 262).

11 Cauchy (1846, 272; translation by Dirk Schlimm).

are also problematic, as they are intended to represent situations that are mathematically impossible. Thus, while mathematical notations share many features with representations, they differ from them in one crucial aspect, namely, that not every expression has to have a referent.

An alternative conception of notations is to consider them as *languages*. After all, we use languages to describe various aspects of the world, but they also have a creative potential of allowing us to make up fictional stories, such as those of Jane Eyre or Sherlock Holmes. The formulation of such stories does not require an ontology in the background and depends essentially on the use of language. Considerations such as these lie behind the philosophical position known as *mathematical fictionalism*.

The conceptualizations of notations as representations and as languages echo a fundamental duality with regard to the main function of mathematical notations, which can be either *descriptive* or *prescriptive*. This duality can also be found in other forms of representations. For example, a system of mathematical axioms can be understood as describing a given subject matter or as defining a class of models;[12] similarly, a painting can depict a real landscape, or it can be purely the product of an artist's imagination. Without having to take a firm stand on whether a notation *re-presents* a given subject matter or *presents* a new subject matter, it is useful to speak of the *intended* subject matter, that is, what a user considers a notation to be about, while keeping in mind that this might be different for different users, and that not every expression must have a referent. Moreover, the intended subject matter might not be clearly defined or understood at all. For example, when Cantor introduced a notation for sets, the concept of set was still in the process of being established and there was no clear delineation about which collections are sets and which are not. Cantor himself is reported to have said, "A set I imagine as an abyss."[13]

In Section 2, we will discuss various aspects of the constituents of mathematical notations (i.e., characters, expressions, and manipulations) in isolation, and then address the use of notations in particular contexts in Section 3. But, before that, some more general considerations about the study of notations are in order.

1.3 The Study of Mathematical Notations

1.3.1 Syntactic and Contextual Approaches to Notations

The conceptualizations of notations as languages and as representations also suggest a distinction between syntactic and other aspects of a notation.

[12] Schlimm (2013).
[13] Ewald (1996, vol. 2, 836).

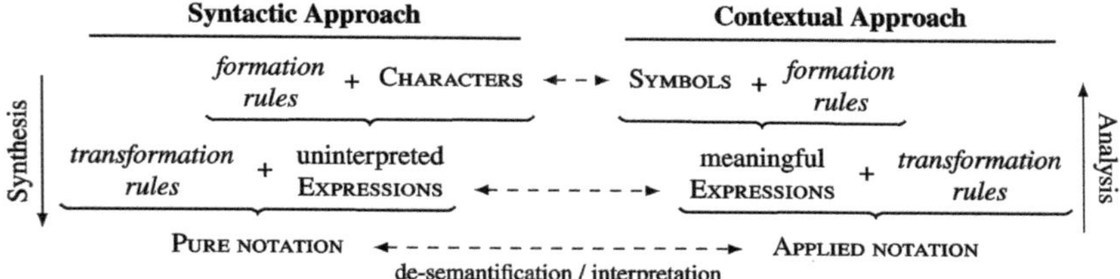

Figure 1 The syntactic and contextual approaches to the study of notations are connected through the processes of interpretation and de-semantification.

As a consequence, we can approach the study of notations from two different points of view, which we might call *syntactic* and *contextual* (Figure 1). Which approach to take depends in large part on the particular questions one is interested in.

In the syntactic approach we begin with a set of meaningless characters, state formation rules for composing them into (uninterpreted) expressions, and rules for transforming them into other expressions. In other words, we synthesize the notational system from its basic components. At each of these stages we can *interpret* (some of) the characters and their arrangements by attributing specific referents to them and thereby turning characters into symbols, uninterpreted expressions into meaningful expressions, and the entire pure notation into an applied notation. Recall, however, that in practice such an interpretation might be only *partial*, yielding a notation in which some expressions have referents and others do not. For example, while '-1' and '$\sqrt{\ }$' were considered meaningful by Cardano, Bombelli, and Cauchy, their combination '$\sqrt{-1}$' was not.

In a contextual approach we typically start with the material inscriptions of a given mathematical notation as it appears, for example, in a mathematical textbook or in a handwritten note. Then, we analyze the way the notation is employed, trying to identify the allowed manipulations, the structure of the expressions, and the basic symbols that are used for their composition. Such an analysis is not necessarily unique, as different manipulations can yield the same results, different formation rules can determine the same class of expressions, and even the identification of the basic symbols need not be uniquely determined. For example, it is not immediately obvious whether '$\neq$' should be considered as a basic symbol or as a combination of the two basic symbols '$=$' and '$/$'. At each stage of this analysis we can try to ignore the context (which includes meanings, practices, and cultural background) in which the notation is used and consider it purely syntactically. This move, which can also be made by the practitioners themselves, has been called 'de-semantification'.[14]

14 Krämer (2003); Dutilh Novaes (2012).

1.3.2 Two Difficulties in the Study of Notations

The tendency of practitioners to favor their own notation, mentioned in the quote by Cajori at the end of Section 1.2.2, poses a great difficulty in the study of notations: the *problem of familiarity*. Typically, users of a notational system spend a considerable time learning it, and developing strategies and shortcuts for manipulating its expressions. It is consequently much easier and faster to use a system one is familiar with, regardless of the intrinsic features of the system. Thus, on the one hand, the familiar system feels intuitive and natural, and, on the other hand, it takes more effort to use an unfamiliar one. An illustration of this phenomenon is John Venn's blunt assessment of Frege's unusual logical notation on the basis of his first impression: "I have not made myself sufficiently familiar with Dr. Frege's system to attempt to work out problems by help of it, but I must confess that it seems to me cumbrous and inconvenient."[15]

What I called the problem of familiarity has been discussed by Tolchinsky, in the context of analyzing writing systems, as the epistemological barrier to being able to imagine other ways of writing and to detach oneself from one's own familiar perspective. She suggests "to see how other systems function" as a way of avoiding this problem.[16]

A second tendency that stands in the way of an unbiased discussion of notations is a *narrow focus* on a single criterion. When looking at two notational systems, it is often the case that one particular difference stands out and this is then taken to be the decisive factor in the comparison; availability and anchoring biases underlie this tendency. For example, the presence of a symbol for zero is one of the more obvious features that distinguish the Indo-Arabic system from the Roman numerals, and this is then sometimes taken to be the *decisive* difference, without further discussion of the actual roles of the symbol for zero.

1.3.3 How to Study Mathematical Notations

To overcome the problems of familiarity and narrow focus, discussions of notations should begin with an analysis of the specific features of the notations in question and then continue with an investigation of how these features relate to aspects of the notations, such as the intended subject matter, users, and tasks. These aspects are discussed in more detail in Section 3. Phrases such as "it is not hard to see" or "it is obvious" might ultimately say more about the author's background and training than about the notation itself. It is therefore extremely

[15] Venn (1880, 237).

[16] Tolchinsky (2003, xxx).

useful to follow Tolchinsky's advice mentioned earlier, namely to familiarize oneself extensively also with alternative notations.

Notations can be studied as they have actually been used by practitioners (in the wild)[17] or, more theoretically, by considering possible uses of them. The former approach poses additional difficulties because people tend to invent idiosyncratic variants, shortcuts, and so on. Motivations behind actual historical developments can sometimes be found in comments by the practitioners themselves, but even these must be taken with a grain of salt as the practitioners might themselves be biased. For the theoretical study of notations, it is advantageous to compare different notations with regard to some specific aspects, while trying to keep the other aspects fixed. Otherwise, if one only looks at a single notation, it is difficult, if not impossible, to determine what actually depends on the notation itself and what depends on the other aspects, such as the intended subject matter.

1.3.4 An Example of the Interplay between Notations and Tasks

To illustrate the study of notations with regard to a particular aspect, here the task of recording a customer's orders, let us consider the following simple scenario: We want to keep track of how many items of a particular kind a customer orders at a bar and determine the total cost, using only a pen and a piece of paper (or a coaster). Three possible ways of proceeding come to mind: First, we could make a tally mark for each ordered item; to obtain the total cost, we have to count the tallies and multiply them by the price of a single item. Second, we could record the price of an item on the coaster each time an item is ordered; at the end of the evening, we would have to add up all individual prices to get the total cost. Third, for each order we could add the price to the previous sum, so that the coaster always indicates the current total. Now, which of these three approaches is the most efficient? This, of course, depends on the dimensions we are interested in, such as (a) the space needed on the coaster, (b) the time to add one more item, which depends on what needs to be computed and written, or (c) the time to determine the total cost. The results of this analysis are shown in Table 1. For adding an item, tallies are best, since they can be written very fast and also take up the least amount of space. However, for computing the final cost, the tallies have to be counted and a multiplication has to be performed. In contrast, when the third algorithm is used, the final result can be read off immediately from the coaster. However, this requires performing an addition each time an item is ordered, so that the effort for adding one more

[17] See Hutchins (1995).

Table 1 Simple example of the interplay of notations and tasks.

	(1) Use tallies	(2) Write items	(3) Write sums
(a) Total space on coaster	little	a lot	a lot
(b) Time for adding item	very fast	fast	slow
(c) Determining total	slow	very slow	immediate

item is considerably greater than with the tallies. To assess some kind of overall efficiency, we would now have to determine some weights for the space and time components.

The upshot of this simple comparison of how three different notations fare at a particular task is that whether a particular notation is *better* than another usually depends on what resources are available (here: coasters and pens), what specific task they are used for, what algorithms are used for these tasks, which dimensions one is mainly interested in, and how the tasks are weighted. The last is often the most contentious question. Changing any of these parameters even slightly can result in a very different assessment: for example, if the task is changed in such a way that different kinds of items with different prices can be ordered, or if the resources are changed to include computations with a pocket calculator.

1.4 Who Is This Element For?

A more thorough understanding of *what* notational systems do and *how* they do it can add another layer of sophistication to philosophical reflections about epistemology and ontology in mathematics and science. Pioneering work in this direction in the philosophy of science was Klein's research on the use of "paper tools" in chemistry.[18] While there have been numerous case studies on the use of notations in mathematics and science since then, in particular by philosophers of mathematical practice,[19] the main purpose of this Element is to lay the groundwork and to sketch the program for a systematic approach to the study of mathematical notations. It is written for everyone who is curious about the world of symbols that surrounds us.

When I taught about the philosophy of notations in the past, I frequently encountered the following pattern: First, students are somewhat skeptical that there is much to say about notations other than some historical facts, for example, who invented what and when. After a while, however, this gives way to

[18] Klein (2002).
[19] See Carter (2024).

an astonished realization that many interesting questions, including traditional philosophical ones, can be asked about notations. Studying the nature of notations and their interrelations with an intended subject matter, their users, and applications, provides us with many opportunities to hone our philosophical skills and to address problems regarding ontology, knowledge, language, history, and thought. In particular, studying notations often requires questioning our intuitive, and sometimes well-entrenched, views in regard to the difference between a subject matter and the way we represent it to ourselves. Addressing the problems of familiarity and narrow focus (Section 1.3.2) requires paying careful attention to details and conceptual distinctions. Some specific questions that should be of interest to philosophers of mathematics and science are discussed in Section 5. Moreover, notations are not only epistemic tools but also *cognitive* tools, so that their study should also benefit cognitive scientists and philosophers of mind, as well as historians and mathematics educators.

Unlike some of the other Elements in this series, which aim at an in-depth discussion of a particular topic, this Element is intended as a general introduction, giving the reader an overview of the field of the philosophy of mathematical notations by introducing the main concepts and terminology for the analysis of notations, and by raising the main questions to be asked. Rather than presenting a particular philosophy of notations (such as Peirce's semiotics), it provides a toolbox and some general suggestions for the further study of mathematical notations. By equipping the reader with methodological and conceptual tools to fruitfully investigate and discuss mathematical notations, this Element will also, hopefully, open up new lines of inquiry for future investigations.

2 Components of Mathematical Notations

In this section we take a closer look at the basic building blocks of mathematical notations, namely, characters and symbols, their structural arrangements, and their manipulations.

2.1 Characters and Symbols

2.1.1 On the Nature of Characters

Regardless of whether we define a notation syntactically or whether we analyze a given mathematical notation, in order to understand and use a notation we must be able to identify what counts as a character and to discriminate the individual characters from each other. In other words, we must be able to identify character tokens (inscriptions) as belonging to different character types. The requirements that allow us to make recognizable copies of the expressions of a notation are identified as *disjointness* and *finite differentiation* by

Goodman (1968). In other words, no inscription may belong to two separate characters, and it must be possible to determine to which character an inscription belongs, if it does at all. Although these requirements might seem trivial at first, they nevertheless rule out the use of certain characters, for example ones that would be defined by their absolute size, as well as notations that have uncountably many characters. Our usual alphabets, numerals, and other symbols typically satisfy these criteria.

As desirable as it would be to have a general context-free definition of characters, this seems impossible, as there is always some degree of background knowledge necessary to individuate them. Even in the case of formal languages the user must know in advance how to identify the characters of the underlying alphabet. In the contextual approach to given mathematical notations, characters can be understood as the smallest syntactic units that make a difference for the way the notation is used. For example, if letters are used differently depending on their colors, then a black and a red letter 'A' constitute two different characters; otherwise, we should consider them as tokens of the same character type. Because of the atomic nature of characters, transformation rules must refer to characters only as a whole and cannot be applied to their parts. This is also the case for composite characters that result from combining different shapes, such as '$\leqq$' and '$\neq$', despite the fact that their shapes might be further decomposed into suggestive elements (e.g., into '$<$' and '$=$').[20] However, whether a particular combination constitutes a single composite character or two individual characters depends on the role of this combination within the mathematical notation system. For example: on the one hand, if adding a prime merely creates new names, such as $a, a', a'', \ldots$, then these are composite characters; on the other hand, if the prime is used to denote the successor function, as in $0, 0', 0'', \ldots$, then '$0'$' is an expression that results from the linear arrangement of the characters '0' and '$'$'.

2.1.2 Cognate Characters

The shapes of characters of a notation can, at least in principle, be chosen arbitrarily. In practice, however, this is rarely the case, as we shall discuss later when looking at the design of notations (Section 4.2.3). Of particular importance in this respect is the use of *cognate characters*. Cognate characters are perceptually similar to each other in ways that are easily recognizable, due to either formal or conventional similarities. These similarities can be exploited

[20] Composite characters differ from complex symbols, which can be decomposed into individual characters (Section 4.2.5).

to suggest some similarity in meaning, thereby yielding considerable cognitive advantages for the use of a notation (Section 4.2.4).

Cognate characters are often related through reflection, rotation, similarity in shape, composition, or by belonging to the same alphabet or font. Size and upper/lower case can be used to further distinguish between cognate characters.

First, the similarities underlying cognate characters can be purely formal. The following table shows some cognate characters that are related by vertical and horizontal *reflections*, as well as *rotations*:

$$\begin{array}{ccccccccc} (& \mathrm{E} & \mathrm{A} & \vee & \bot & \cup & \& & \& & + \\ ) & \exists & \forall & \wedge & \top & \cap & ⅋ & ⅋ & \times \end{array}$$

Cognate characters can also be similar in *shape*:

$$) \quad \} \quad] \qquad \vee \quad \cup \quad \mathrm{U} \qquad \approx \quad = \quad \equiv \qquad + \quad \dagger \quad \cdot|\cdot$$

Formal similarities can also exist between composite characters:

$$\bar{A} \quad \dot{A} \quad A' \quad A_1 \quad A^2 \quad {}^3A \quad {}_4A$$

$$\bar{\delta} \quad \dot{\delta} \quad \delta' \quad \delta_1 \quad \delta^2 \quad {}^3\delta \quad {}_4\delta$$

These examples also illustrate how characters can be cognate to others in more than one way: We easily recognize that both the characters in the rows in the preceding display and the characters in the columns are cognate.

Second, in addition to the purely perceptual similarities between characters, characters can also be cognate on the basis of some well-established conventions, such as belonging to the same typographical family, like the letters of an alphabet or the digits of a system of numerals. Characters that differ in one of the parameters that are used in defining typefaces are also usually recognized as bearing some kind of similarity to each other, even if they appear in different fonts, weights, letter cases, or even alphabets. For example, consider the following characters:

$$\begin{array}{cccccc} \mathrm{A} & A & \mathrm{a} & \mathbf{a} & \mathfrak{A} & \alpha \\ \mathrm{B} & B & \mathrm{b} & \mathbf{b} & \mathfrak{B} & \beta \\ \mathrm{C} & C & \mathrm{c} & \mathbf{c} & \mathfrak{C} & \gamma \end{array}$$

The characters in a column are cognate, because they belong to the same alphabet, case, font, and so on, but the characters in a row are also cognate, because they are different representations of the same letters.[21] Thus, just as we have seen with the examples of composite characters, basic characters can also be

[21] This remark assumes that it makes sense to speak of the *same* letters across different alphabets, such as the Latin and Greek alphabets.

related to each other in various ways that are independent of each other. This allows us to further establish various layers of similarities, which is a feature often used in mathematical notations. For example, in the following general form of a circle equation,

$$x^2 + y^2 - Ax - By - C = 0,$$

we can easily distinguish the letters that appear in lower case from those that appear in upper case and attribute different meanings to them: by convention, the lower-case letters (x, y) are *variables* and the upper-case letters (A, B, C) are the *parameters* of the equation. (Historically, the use of parameters instead of fixed values was introduced by Vieta in 1591 and the convention of using letters from the end of the alphabet as variables was introduced by Descartes in 1637.)

2.2 Structured Expressions

In order to form an expression in a notation, the characters must be arranged in such a way that we can recognize the result as a well-formed expression. Syntactically, this can be achieved by explicitly stating *formation rules*, but in practice these are often left implicit and communicated through examples, which leaves plenty of room for ambiguities and notational variants.

Regarding the arrangements of characters, a distinction is sometimes made in the literature between one- and two-dimensional notations, for example, to distinguish sentential from diagrammatic notations. However, I consider this terminology to be more problematic than useful. After all, every inscription must be two-dimensional to be visible to the eye, and even typical sentential expressions extend spatially in two dimensions, for example, using sub- or superscripts. More fruitful for the discussion of notations is the distinction between linear and non-linear notations, as well as the methods of grouping, ordering, and nesting.

2.2.1 Linear Notations

The most common way of arranging symbols into expressions is by simply *concatenating* them to form a *string* of characters. This procedure is very familiar, because this is how we commonly join letters to form words, and words to form sentences. In general, however, not every string that can be formed from a set of characters will count as a well-formed expression, just as not every concatenation of letters forms an English word. Thus, the composition of expressions is usually restricted by explicit or implicit formation rules. When learning a given mathematical notation, extracting these formation rules from examples is a crucial, but sometimes difficult, prerequisite for using it correctly.

Expressions that are obtained purely by concatenation are *linear* or *sequential*. In a linear expression that consists of more than one symbol token, every symbol has at most two adjacent symbols, and exactly two symbols (called *end symbols*) have only one adjacent symbol. This allows us to parse a linear expression in two unique ways by beginning with one of the end symbols and moving from one adjacent symbol to the next; typical reading conventions limit the parsing to a single direction. Here are three examples of linear expressions that could be found in a mathematical text:

$$(12 + 2)i \qquad 3.14 \times 10^{(10^{10})} + 4 \qquad x_{27} - y_5 = 0.$$

We immediately notice in the second and third examples that a linear expression can extend spatially in different directions through the use of subscripts or superscripts. Nevertheless, for parsing a linear notation correctly it is sufficient to individuate symbol occurrences and to understand adjacency (here as 'immediately to the left of' and 'immediately to the right of') as the result of concatenation.

By extending the repertoire of characters and spatial relations in which they can be arranged, we can obtain quite complex layouts. For example, we can add curves as characters together with the relation 'encloses,' so that the characters do not need to be written next to each other, but can also be used around each other. In this case, the following can also be an expression in a linear notation:

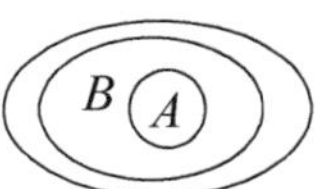

For a linear reading of expressions that are based on the relations *immediately to the right of* and *encloses* to be possible, a vertical stacking of subexpressions must be excluded, because otherwise we could not determine which of these is to the right of the other.

2.2.2 Non-linear Notations

If the symbols are arranged in such a way that there is not a unique predecessor and successor for each symbol, the notation is *non-linear*. For example:

$$x_3^2 \qquad \frac{3x + 4}{x} \qquad \sum_{i=0}^{n} i.$$

In these expressions it is possible to move through all symbols from different starting points and in different directions. Examples of more complex non-linear notations are diagrams (discussed later in Section 3.1.3) and tabular arrangements, such as matrices.[22] As is to be expected, these additional degrees of freedom bring with them some advantages and disadvantages: notations of this kind typically use fewer characters and are thus easier to parse at a glance; but the lack of designated end symbols and the fact that there is not a unique parsing order can also make them more difficult to parse, especially if the expressions are more complex (in such cases, the use of variable-length symbols and symbol size can be used to perceptually structure the expressions as illustrated in the second and third examples at the beginning of this section).

By the addition of parentheses or rearranging the symbols, non-linear notations can be *syntactically linearized*:

$$(x_3)^2 \qquad (3x+4)/x \qquad \Sigma_{i=0}{}^{n}\ i.$$

Alternatively, non-linear notations can also be *pragmatically linearized* by the addition of *reading conventions*; for example, by requiring that in the case of the presence of both subscripts and superscripts, the former are to be read first. When discussing such notations, however, we should consider them as two different, but related, notations, one non-linear and the other linear.

2.2.3 Grouping

If a notation is used to represent operations of some kind, it is often necessary to distinguish the order in which these operations are performed; for example, if an operation is not associative (like material implication in propositional logic) or different operations are used (like addition and multiplication). Grouping can be achieved by characters and their arrangement, or by conventions. In our familiar logical and algebraic notations we typically use *parentheses* for grouping:

$$A \to (B \to C) \quad \text{vs.} \quad (A \to B) \to C, \qquad 3 + (4 \times 2) \quad \text{vs.} \quad (3+4) \times 2.$$

With the use of *conventions* for binding and operator precedence, such as left-associativity or PEMDAS (parentheses, exponents, multiplication/division, addition/subtraction), some of the parentheses can be dispensed with, but not all. For example, with these conventions the preceding expressions can be simplified to the following:

$$A \to (B \to C) \quad \text{vs.} \quad A \to B \to C, \qquad 3 + 4 \times 2 \quad \text{vs.} \quad (3+4) \times 2.$$

If such conventions are used, the number of symbols in an expression is reduced at the cost of more complex parsing rules that have to be memorized.

22 Schlimm (2022).

Alternative means of grouping subexpressions in a linear notation are the use of dots and over- or underlines (vincula), as in

$$3 + 4\,.\times 2 \qquad \text{and} \qquad \overline{3 + 4} \times 2.$$

Instead of introducing an extra character just for the grouping, symbols of *variable length* can also be used for grouping subexpressions, such as circles, the vinculum for fractions, or the common symbol for root extraction. For example:

$$\frac{3 + 4}{2} \qquad \sqrt{3 + 4} \times 2.$$

2.2.4 Order of Operations and Arguments

In the previous examples, the binary operator symbols were always written between their arguments, which is called *infix* notation. Alternatively, they can also be put in front or behind their arguments, resulting in the so-called *prefix* (Polish) or *postfix* (reverse Polish) notations. For example, $5 + 12$ is represented in prefix and postfix notations by

$$+\ 5\ 12 \qquad \text{and} \qquad 5\ 12\ +.$$

Because here the subexpressions all have the same form, namely an operation symbol followed by two arguments (or two arguments followed by an operation symbol), these notations do not require any parentheses or other means of grouping. This generally reduces the number of characters in an expression. For example, $(5 + 12) \times 7$ is represented by

$$\times + 5\ 12\ 7 \qquad \text{and} \qquad 5\ 12 + 7\ \times.$$

in prefix and postfix notation, respectively. These notations have various practical advantages in certain tasks, which was the reason for them being used as input format for various computers and pocket calculators (e.g., they require fewer button presses and allow for computations using a stack). However, we also notice the need for some means other than the operation symbol (here, space) to separate the arguments from each other.

The order in which operations and arguments are represented can also impose restrictions on the number of arguments: an infix notation works well for binary operations, since one argument appears in front of the operation symbol and the other after it, but it cannot be easily generalized to more arguments. The prefix (and postfix) notations, on the other hand, can be applied to more than two arguments, e.g., $+\ 1\ 2\ 3\ 4 = 10$. As long as the number of arguments is kept fixed, nothing changes. However, if the arity of the operation is variable, then the form of subexpressions is no longer fixed and it becomes necessary to indicate which arguments belong to which operation, thereby eliminating the advantage that these notations do not require other means of grouping.

2.2.5 Nested Notations

As we have already seen in some of the expressions shown earlier, mathematical notations sometimes make use of expressions of *other* notational systems to form their own expressions. In particular, numerals and primes are often used as subscripts or superscripts if one wants to express an ordering or simply have an unlimited supply of symbols. For example, the first derivative of f is often written as f', the second as f''. This works well, as long as only the first few derivatives are used: they can be read at a glance and it avoids the ambiguity caused by using superscripts to indicate powers. Similar cumulative notations were also used by Leibniz to indicate different quantities, such as $n, (n), ((n)), \ldots$.[23] If more items are needed, say for variable names, constant symbols, or function symbols, then numerals are often used as subscripts (as in x_0, A_3, and $f_2(x)$). What can easily be overlooked in these examples is that here the main use of the numerals is not to represent numbers, but to syntactically disambiguate different variables. This becomes obvious when noticing that no numerical properties of such subscripts are being used (the subscripts are not added, etc.), which is similar to using numerals as phone numbers or as names for bank accounts. This is not to say that subscripts cannot be used as numerals: in the formulation of the recursion theorem, $\varphi_{f(n)} = \varphi_n$, they are, in fact, used in this way.

Another example of nesting notations is the use of set-theoretic expressions within other notational systems, such as for logic, as in $\forall x \in \mathbb{N}: x = x$. Such nestings of notations typically allow for concise notations and are straightforward for experienced users, but can be difficult for novices.

2.2.6 Variants and Families of Notations

The individuation of mathematical notations can be difficult, in particular when they are not given syntactically, but only through examples. For a most fine-grained analysis, if two notational systems differ in some feature that makes a difference in how they are used, then we should consider them as different notations. For example, when writing long numerals people often group the digits into smaller groups: Fibonacci (1202) used arcs to partition the numerals, $(\widehat{982}721)$; Tonstall (1522) used dots $(98\dot{2}721)$;[24] the German DIN-5008 norm suggests using spaces or periods (982.721); in English, it is common to

[23] Knobloch (2016, 233).

[24] See Cajori (1928a, 58–59).

use commas (982,721). While this practice does not change the number that is being represented, it does dramatically increase readability and verbalization (more on this in Section 3.2). Nevertheless, there are many features that these notations have in common, which suggests to consider them to be *variants*.

Notational variation can be achieved in different ways, which can also be combined with each other: (a) *Syntactic variants* arise by replacing some characters by others. (b) *Augmented variants* result from adding blank spaces, parentheses, colors, and so on to a notation. (c) In *reduced variants* certain characters, such as parentheses or operation symbols, are omitted, mainly to shorten the expressions and avoid clutter; this is often achieved by introducing conventions.

Notational variants that have underlying structural principles in common are frequently classified together as *families* of notational systems. In the case of numeral systems, for example, nearly every notational system relies on some way of representing the powers of a *base* and the *multiples* of these powers (and possibly also multiples of a subbase). In our familiar decimal place-value system, the base-powers are indicated by the position (place) in the expression, while the multipliers are represented by the digits. Other systems that are built on these same principles can also be considered to belong to the family of *positional* systems, such as the binary system and the Babylonian sexagesimal system. Developing such classifications of notational systems is an important task in the philosophy of notations and it is discussed further in Section 5.2.1.

2.2.7 Conventions

Conventions are an essential, but thorny, ingredient for the use of many notations. Like the formation and manipulation rules of a mathematical notation, they pose a special kind of difficulty in the study of notations because of their immaterial nature. After all, one cannot look at a notation and see the conventions. Rather, either they have to be known explicitly by the user, or they have to be extrapolated from the way a notation is used. Thus, on the one hand, they add to the cognitive load necessary for using a notation, in particular for novices. On the other hand, they can also reduce the cognitive load by reducing the length and complexity of expressions, by strengthening the associations between syntactic and semantic elements (as in the example of grouping numerals shown in the previous section), and by being applicable in different notational systems.

We can distinguish between *semantic* and *pragmatic* conventions. The former are crucial for the proper understanding of expressions, such as the conventions mentioned earlier regarding associativity and operator precedence (Section 2.2.3), which were introduced to reduce the number of parentheses in an expression. Conventions of this kind are, in a sense, similar to the formation rules of expressions (see Figure 1) and so they must be considered as constitutive elements of a notational system. Pragmatic conventions can facilitate the reading and general use of a notation but do not affect the meaning of the expressions. For example, the consistent use of letters at the end of the alphabet for variables (x, y, z) and of letters at the beginning of the alphabet for constants (a, b, c) across different notational systems makes them easier to use, because knowledge about one system can be transferred to another. Conventions can also be both semantic and pragmatic. The dropping of outer parentheses of expressions, for example, affects which expressions are considered to be well-formed, but is also employed both in algebra and in logic.

2.3 Manipulations

2.3.1 Manipulations as Characteristic for Mathematical Notations

The considerations discussed so far apply to notational systems in a very general sense, including those that are intended to be merely representational, such as musical scores and notations for dancing. What distinguishes mathematical, or operational, notations from these is that they are also intended to be manipulated in such a way that new insights about the subject matter can be obtained through the transformation of expressions into others. For example, we can use numerals not only to represent quantities, but also to perform calculations; we can use equations not only to express relations between quantities, but also to obtain new relations through algebraic manipulations; we can use logical formulas not only to represent logical relations, but also to formulate proofs; and so on. It is this availability of rules for manipulating expressions that underlies mathematical reasoning, according to Babbage's *On the influence of signs in mathematical reasoning* (1826). Manipulations are also crucial in more recent discussions of notations as "epistemic actions," "paper tools," and underlying "thinking in symbols."[25]

Not all notations used in mathematics are operative, even if they are used in proofs. Diagrams are an illustrative example. On the one hand, there are diagrams that are used mainly to visualize relations between various entities: once they are set up, they are read or "chased," for example, in category theory. This can be fruitful for revealing or justifying hitherto unknown relationships, but the diagrams themselves are not necessarily transformed further into others. In Euclidean geometry, on the other hand, diagrams themselves are manipulated in the course of a proof, so that they are indeed mathematical notations in the operative sense.

[25] See De Cruz and De Smedt (2010), Klein (2001), and Tolchinsky (2003).

In principle, it is also possible to manipulate notations that were originally intended to be only representational. For example, Bach famously applied syntactic transformations on notation for music in some of his compositions, and it is not difficult to imagine a choreographer inventing new dance moves on the basis of a notation for dancing. Thus, we can consider the notion of an operative notation to come in degrees, or simply speak of *mathematical uses* of notations that are generally not used in this way. Notice that in these cases the manipulations could yield expressions that fail to denote elements of the intended subject matter, either because they cannot be played on an instrument or because they would require one to overcome the limitations of how human bodies can move. This observation further supports the argument made in Section 1.2.4 that mathematical notations are not purely representational.

2.3.2 Agglomerative and Discursive Manipulations

The example of Euclidean diagrams as a mathematical notation suggests a principled distinction we can draw between two different kinds of manipulations. Following the terminology introduced by Stenning, we call them *agglomerative* and *discursive* modes of reasoning.[26] Reasoning is agglomerative, if an expression is transformed into another through direct alteration, for example, when a line is added to a given diagram; discursive reasoning, on the other hand, generates a new, distinct expression from a given one, for example, when the equation $x = 2 + 3$ is simplified to $x = 5$. The outcomes of these manipulations are, in the first case, a single expression (namely the augmented diagram), and, in the second case, two expressions (namely, '$x = 2 + 3$' and '$x = 5$'). Thus, discursive reasoning keeps a history of the outcomes of performed manipulations, whereas agglomerative reasoning only yields the final resulting expression. In principle, however, any agglomerative sequence of reasoning steps can be represented discursively as a series of individual steps.

2.3.3 Efficiency Depends on Resources and Algorithms

The ease and efficiency with which manipulations can be carried out in a notation is often used as the main criterion of its assessment (see Section 4.3.2). A fact that is often overlooked in the literature and is thus worth emphasizing here, is that, in addition to the structure of the notation, computational efficiency also depends on the available *computational resources*. For example,

[26] Stenning (2000, 2002).

the Indo-Arabic decimal system has been developed for human use, but most digital computers represent numbers nowadays in a binary system. The latter is indeed a matter of efficiency of implementation and not a necessity due to the digital nature of computers: historically, some computers were built with a decimal system for the representation of numbers, such as the ENIAC and the IBM 702.[27] Thus, any meaningful comparison of notational systems in terms of their computational efficiency must take into consideration the computational resources that are used and, ideally, be made on the basis of a common set of *basic operations*. The particular choice of such operations, however, can also affect the outcome of the comparison, in particular, if the notations were not originally designed to be manipulated by the operations in question.

Even with a fixed set of basic operations, manipulations can generally be carried out according to different *algorithms*, which can dramatically affect the efficiency of the manipulations. For example, if one searches sequentially for an entry in an old-fashioned phone book page by page, this is considerably less effective than performing a binary search (i.e., opening the book in the middle and repeating this procedure in the half that contains the desired entry). These particular algorithms can also be studied theoretically using *complexity theory*, resulting in the two different complexity classes of linear and logarithmic time complexity. However, in general, the concepts of complexity theory are too coarse to allow for a meaningful comparison of algorithms that are used by human beings. In particular, humans apply manipulations only to data of a relatively small size, whereas statements about complexity classes are typically 'in the limit.'[28]

With experience, humans are often quite ingenious in coming up with shortcuts and more efficient ways of performing symbolic manipulations. Just ask several people (especially mathematicians) how exactly they perform certain mental calculations, and you might be surprised by the variety of different answers you will get. Moreover, efficient algorithms for specific tasks can be different from those used in everyday life: For example, a method recommended for performing quick mental additions in *Miracle Math* (1992) proceeds from left to right.[29] Thus, human subjects might vary considerably when performing certain tasks that involve notations, depending on whether the subjects are novices or experts, and on their overall familiarity with the notations in question. Because of the difficulty involved in controlling for all of

27 Haigh and Ceruzzi (2021, 14 and 57).

28 See Pantsar (2021) for different notions of cognitive and computational complexity.

29 Lorayne (1992).

these factors, experimental work on the efficiency of notations in actual practice is rare and we are often left only with anecdotes and questionable arguments.

3 Mathematical Notations in Practice

In the previous section, the building blocks of mathematical notations (characters and their arrangement into expressions, and manipulations on them) were presented outside of any particular context of use. We now relate these components to aspects that arise in practical contexts.

Figure 2 shows an overview of the six main aspects of notations that we shall consider in each of the following subsections: (1) the *subject matter* (semantics), (2) *verbalization* (language), (3) *users* and their resources (cognition), (4) *tasks* (applications), (5) the *material* basis, and (6) the *tradition* or historical context (other notations). The arrows in the figure indicate the main connections between these aspects, although there are also others. Each individual use of a notation in practice can influence and be influenced by any and all of the aspects. This can make the analysis of notations somewhat confusing and unsystematic, if one does not make the effort first to treat these aspects separately, consider their trade-offs, and then weigh their relevance for a particular application.

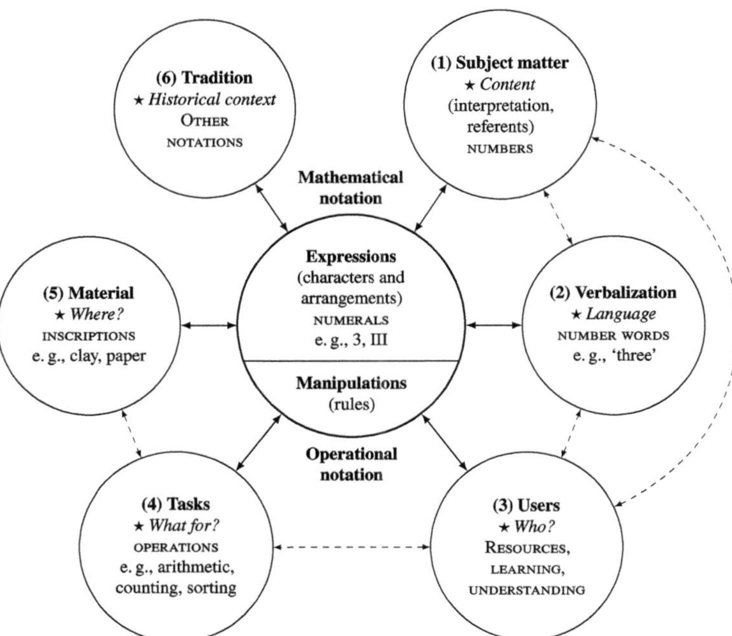

Figure 2 Aspects of mathematical notations in practice.

3.1 Subject Matter and Primitives

3.1.1 Notational Elements and Their Meanings

Relating a notation, namely a set of structured expressions, to an intended subject matter involves two main steps: First, we must identify relevant *primitives* of the intended subject matter, which can be objects, concepts, relations, operations, and so on. Second, we must map these primitives to the notational elements, that is, to the characters and their arrangements.

To make the primitives and the mapping explicit, it is useful to represent the relation between the notational elements and the intended subject matter in a table, as shown for algebraic expressions, such as '$(y \times x) + y$', in Table 2.

In some cases, a primitive can be mapped directly to a notational element, but in most cases some more complex, and often recursive, rules are necessary. In the previous example the use of parentheses is tied to the infix arrangement of the operators and applies also to subexpressions. Such rules are also called the *syntax* of the notation. Thus, in many cases a simple table can only be a first approximation. Nevertheless, starting the analysis of a notation in this way is a good practice for getting clear about and making explicit the relations between the notational elements and their role in relating to an intended subject matter.

What we should keep in mind is that choosing a notation always involves conceptualizing the subject matter in a certain way and thereby possibly also imposes certain restrictions on it and on the use of the notation itself. For example, deciding to represent arithmetical addition by '+' using infix notation, as shown earlier, implies a conception of addition as a binary operation (because only two terms 'x' and 'y' can be arranged in this way as '$x + y$') and requires some way of grouping (e.g., with parentheses) and laws of associativity to represent the addition of three terms. However, in principle, addition could also

Table 2 Mapping between notational elements and intended subject matter for simple algebraic expressions, such as '$(y \times x) + y$'.

NOTATIONAL ELEMENTS		INTENDED SUBJECT MATTER
Characters	**Arrangements**	**Primitives**
lowercase letters		variables
+	linear, infix	addition
×	linear, infix	multiplication
parentheses		order of operations

be conceptualized as an n-ary operation without any intrinsic order among the terms, for example, written as $\sum\{x_1,\ldots,x_n\}$ – although this might not occur naturally to us due to our familiarity with the notation that represents it as a binary operation (see Section 1.3.2). Then again, writing several addends underneath each other, as is often done in paper-and-pencil computations, might also be closer to a conception of addition as an n-ary operation.

The choice of primitives might seem straightforward in a clear and well-defined domain (e.g., if we are looking for a notation to represent whether a key on a piano is pressed or not) or for those notations that we are already familiar with, but it is much less so when we are dealing with new and abstract material. Examples from the development of symbolic logic illustrate the variety of choices: Boole (1854) represented the propositional connectives conjunction, disjunction, and negation in his notation, while Frege (1879) chose negation and the conditional as basic; Sheffer (1913) and Nicod (1917) famously used only a single binary connective (NOR and NAND, respectively),[30] and in a contemporary presentation of propositional logic we often find a redundant set of primitives, namely, negation, conjunction, disjunction, conditional, and the biconditional being used.[31] There are good reasons for each of these choices, but none of them is dictated by the intended subject matter. Rather, it is the particular tasks that one wants to employ the notation for that justify the choice of primitives.

As the previous example of algebraic expressions also illustrates, the particular structure of a notation might itself influence the number and kind of primitives that are chosen. For a different example, if the natural numbers are presented in the Indo-Arabic decimal place-value notation, we need ten different numbers (the numbers from zero to nine) to be represented by an individual symbol and we use the position in the numeral expression to represent the powers of the base; but in a tally notation only two primitives suffice: the number one and the operation of addition, represented by '|' and concatenation, respectively. In the way natural numbers are often represented in formal logic, the primitives consist of zero and the successor function, yielding the sequence of expressions: 0, S0, SS0, SSS0, and so on.[32] Note that in the last example concatenation does not represent addition, but the application of the successor function.

The previous examples also show that some primitives are represented by characters, while others are represented by the way the characters are arranged

[30] As Elkind and Zach (2023, 27) found out, this work was anticipated by Stamm (1911).

[31] See, for example, Enderton (2001, 14).

[32] See, for example, Enderton (2001, 187–188).

(such as concatenation and the position in a string). Further analysis of the relations between notational elements and intended subject matter reveals that every relevant primitive must be represented in a notation, but neither must every primitive correspond to a unique notational element, nor must every notational element correspond to a unique primitive. In other words, a primitive can be represented by more than one notational element, and a notational element can stand for none, one, or more than one primitive element of the subject matter: the mapping between primitives and notational elements does not need to be one-to-one. That some notations use different characters and arrangements to represent the same primitive illustrates the first claim. For example, in the expression '$2 \cdot 3x$', multiplication is represented both by the character '$\cdot$' and by the juxtaposition of '3' and 'x'. These different uses might express a difference between the kinds of factors (e.g., two numbers, or a number and a variable) or a difference in the order of precedence. To illustrate the second claim, characters can also be notational elements that serve only the purpose of providing a framework for the relative positioning of other characters, such as the horizontal lines (staff) in contemporary musical notation. In addition, characters can also be used for two different purposes: in the expression '$\sqrt{3+x}+4$', for example, the variable-length radical symbol '$\sqrt{}$' indicates both the operation of taking the root and its scope, that is, the grouping together of the radicand '$3+x$'. Similarly, in the analysis of the Roman numeral system presented in Section 5.2.1, an occurrence of 'C' indicates both the value 100 and the fact that this value is to be taken once, so that two occurrences stand for 200.

3.1.2 Expressions and Their Meanings

The nature of the relation between expressions and their intended subject matter is the topic in the philosophy of notations that has received by far the most attention from philosophers. In particular, the works of Peirce and Goodman have been very influential, so that they deserve a brief discussion. But let me first point out some differences between their approach and the present one: First, both Peirce and Goodman consider meanings (conceived mainly as referents) to be constitutive for a notational system, and, second, both consider the intended subject matter to be neatly partitioned and given independently from the notation. Thus, for them, notations are representations, and they do not consider the possibility of expressions having no referents (see Section 1.2.4).

Peirce and Iconicity

Charles Sanders Peirce carried out one of the first and most influential studies on the relation between signs and their meanings, which developed into the field of semiotics, and, as we saw, he also coined the phrase 'philosophy of notation.' Peirce's fundamental notion is that of a *sign*, which is very broad, encompassing anything that can stand for anything else, ranging from the smoke of a fire, over individual letters, to differential equations. He characterized such signs as *symbols*, *indices*, and *icons*, depending on how they relate to their referents, but these are not mutually exclusive. For Peirce, symbols are arbitrary and conventional, and they allow for the generality of signs. (Note that this terminology is different from that introduced in Section 1.3.1, according to which a symbol is a meaningful character, regardless of the nature and origin of its meaning.) Indices, for Peirce, are signs that are "really connected,"[33] for example in a physical way, to their objects, and they determine the subject of a discourse; finally, icons are mainly characterized as signs that resemble their objects. For Peirce, this resemblance underlies our use of signs as a calculus and our ability to reason with them. Moreover, the relation of resemblance can be so strong as to make it difficult to distinguish the sign from the object it denotes, as in the case of geometric diagrams.

While Peirce's further extensive and idiosyncratic reflections about signs have remained mainly a topic for Peirce scholars, his notion of *iconicity* has become a staple in the discussion of notations. Some cases are fairly obvious, for example, that the expressions '☺' and ':-)' resemble a human face, albeit invoking different primitives (namely, contour, eyes, and mouth in the first, and eyes, nose, and mouth in the second). However, how a character or an expression, such as '3' or 'III', can *resemble* an abstract subject matter, such as the number three, is less clear. Different ways of fleshing out the notion of iconicity have been proposed to account for the relation between signs and their objects, including operational iconicity, resemblance in qualities, resemblance in structure, indirect resemblance, exemplar iconicity, and systematic iconicity.[34] The idea behind operational iconicity is that more information can be extracted from an expression than was necessary to construct it.[35] This has been further elaborated by Shimojima in the context of diagrams under the label 'free ride.'[36]

Goodman and Isomorphism

Nelson Goodman's seminal *Languages of Art* (1968) has not sparked the same amount of research as Peirce's writings, but it had a substantial impact on the

33 Peirce (1885, 181).
34 See Schlimm (2021) for an overview.
35 See Stjernfelt (2007, 90–92).
36 Shimojima (2015).

philosophical study of symbolic notations nonetheless. His discussion had both positive and negative effects on the further study of notations: On the one hand, Goodman offered a sharp theoretical analysis of the notion of a notational system. On the other hand, he explicitly excluded certain aspects of notations from his analysis, such as maneuverability and graphic suggestiveness, as being merely "engineering matters," although admitting that these might be "to some degree even necessary for any practicable notation" and their study possibly "fascinating and profitable."[37] The aim of his own investigations was to establish criteria that "are categorically required for any even theoretically workable notational system."[38]

According to Goodman, a notational *scheme* consists of *characters* (which are classes of *inscriptions*) and *modes* of combining them. In the terminology introduced in Section 1.2.3 a scheme corresponds to a notational system, but for Goodman such a scheme becomes a notational *system* only if it is correlated to a *field of reference*, that is, a class of things that the notation is about. To focus his investigation, Goodman turns his attention toward what he considers to be the *primary function* of notational systems. For the case of a musical score, for example, he identifies the primary function as "the authoritative identification of a work from performance to performance,"[39] while considering facilitating transposition, comprehension, or compositions only as secondary functions. Thus, a score must define all of its instantiations and provide means to mark off those performances that do not instantiate it. For this to be possible at all, Goodman identifies five criteria that any notational system must satisfy: it must be unambiguous, and satisfy *disjointness* and *finite differentiation*, both with regard to its characters (syntactically) and its field of reference (semantically). Ultimately, for a notational system to work, Goodman requires a one-to-one correspondence (isomorphism) between characters and their referents (classes of objects). While he captures crucial aspects of characters in his analysis (see Section 2.1.1), Goodman's general approach, which derives by and large from his analysis of notations in music and art, does not fit too well to mathematical notations, which are not purely representational and where the manipulation of expressions is an integral part.

3.1.3 Diagrams

A special and frequently discussed kind of mathematical notation is *diagrams*. These are often characterized as consisting in essential ways of line or curve

[37] Goodman (1968, 155).
[38] Goodman (1968, 156).
[39] Goodman (1968, 128).

segments, or as simply being two-dimensional, but more sophisticated characterizations have also been proposed in the literature.[40] However, we do not need to settle on an exact definition of what constitutes a diagram here, as all of these characterizations can be fitted under our conception of a notation as a systematic set of expressions consisting of arrangements of characters. Also, further taxonomies of diagrams that have been proposed, for example, in terms of whether geometric and topological features of the arrangement are considered, can easily be accommodated, and properties attributed to diagrams, such as overspecificity or allowing for free rides, can be carried over to notations.[41] For the sake of our discussion we can consider diagrams to be those notational systems that have lines, open or closed curves, or arrows as characters, which are typically, though not necessarily, arranged in a non-linear fashion. In general, diagrams seem to have a greater variability among the inscriptions that are recognized as belonging to the same character type than, say, letters. A more detailed analysis of diagrams certainly deserves its own, separate treatment, so we shall consider them here only as particular examples of mathematical notations.

It is worth pointing out that our characterization of notations also includes ones that have both letters and graphical elements as characters. For example, Euclidean diagrams with letters as labels for some points or lines can be seen as a nested notational system. Other notations, such as Cheng's *truth diagrams* and the *bracket notation* for knots,[42] have caused some bewilderment among philosophers ("more like hieroglyphics, a form of picture writing"),[43] but in our treatment of notations they do not pose any particular difficulties. For example, the bracket polynomial

$$\langle \times \rangle = A\langle\,)(\,\rangle + A^{-1}\langle \asymp \rangle$$

is simply an expression of a linear notation in which some of the characters are more graphic and iconic than others.

3.1.4 Notational Artifacts

So far, we have focused mainly on the fit between a notation and its intended subject matter, but there are also important issues arising from a mismatch

40 See, for example, the articles in Allwein and Barwise (1996), and Stenning (2000). Some confusion in the literature arises from Peirce's use of the term 'diagram' for some iconic representations, because his notion also encompasses linear symbolic notations, for example, algebraic formulas.

41 See, for example, De Toffoli (2023, 13) and Carter (2021).

42 See Cheng (2020) and Kauffman (2001, 28 ff.).

43 Brown (2008, 93).

between these two. In particular, some design choices can have unintended implications for the mapping between a notation and its intended subject matter, giving rise to *notational artifacts*.

Parentheses can be seen as notational artifacts that arise from using a linear notation together with an infix arrangement of operations and arguments (Sections 2.2.1 and 2.2.4). A pair of matching parentheses does not have an independent meaning in terms of the intended subject matter, but they are necessary for certain notations to establish a correct mapping between subexpressions and the order in which operations are carried out. This order can be represented without the use of parentheses in non-linear notations or in linear notations with a prefix ordering. Notational artifacts typically augment the total number of characters in an expression, potentially cluttering it up, but they can also enhance the readability of expressions, for example, when parentheses of different sizes or shapes are used.

The choice of a linear notation not only makes parentheses necessary in some cases, but also imposes an order on the symbols in an expression: two symbols 'X' and 'Y' have to appear as either 'XY' or 'YX'. Because of this, we get two different arithmetical expressions '$3 + 5$' and '$5 + 3$', and two logical formulas '$A \wedge B$' and '$B \wedge A$', for which the question arises whether they have the same meaning or not. That the subject matter of logic does not unequivocally settle the question is made manifest by Peirce's Existential Graph notation, in which a closed curve ('cut') indicates the negation of what is inside the curve and juxtaposition represents conjunction.[44] Here, the logical expressions 'AB', 'BA', and '$\substack{A\\B}$' are read as different tokens of the *same* expression type, which denotes the conjunction of A and B. Thus, we notice that the question of whether an aspect of a notation is intended, whether it is a free ride, or whether it is an artifact, is not always easy to determine, in particular when we consider only a single notational system. Taking alternative notations into consideration can help in clarifying the issue. We return to this philosophical matter in Section 5.1.2, noting here that in contemporary mathematics and logic, the expressions shown previously are usually treated as *different* and as requiring a proof of their equivalence. This, however, is not the only way to deal with a situation where the ordering of terms appears as a notational artifact. In an informal treatment of set theory, for example, it is clear from the understanding of the intended subject matter that the two expressions '$\{a, b\}$' and '$\{b, a\}$' stand for the *same* set. In other words, the ordering on the elements that is imposed by the linearity of the notation is considered an artifact that

[44] Interpreted as an Existential Graph, the rightmost expression shown in Section 1.2.3 can be read as the logical formula: $\neg(A \wedge B \wedge \neg(B \wedge \neg C))$. See also Figure 4 for other examples.

is not mathematically relevant. In terms of the type/token distinction, we can express this by saying that '$\{a,b\}$' and '$\{b,a\}$' (just as the Existential Graphs '*AB*' and '*BA*') are interpreted as two tokens of the same formula type, but that in contemporary logic '$A \wedge B$' and '$B \wedge A$' are tokens of two different formula types.

Over time, notational artifacts can also have an effect on the intended subject matter itself. For example, the introduction of the number zero is intimately connected with the use of notational artifacts that had been in use long before the view emerged that they actually represent a number. The most common versions of a place-value system allow for 'empty' places to indicate powers of the base that do not factor in the value of the represented number. For example, in one of the oldest place-value systems, the ancient Babylonian base-60 system, these places were initially simply marked by a space.[45] While we might be inclined to disparage this practice for its potential to lead to ambiguity, it persisted nonetheless for several centuries until a particular placeholder character was introduced to mark an empty place. This character was clearly a notational artifact, since it had no independent numerical meaning and was only used within the notation to indicate the lack of specific factors. In our familiar Indo-Arabic notation this role is played by the symbol '0', which we now also use to represent a number, for example, the result of subtracting 3 from 3. However, these two roles are independent of each other and they do not have to be played by the same symbol.[46] Indeed, while the Babylonians used a symbol to mark empty places, they had no symbol to mark the individual number zero, and in Digges' *Stratioticus* (1579) we find the symbol '$\circ$' used within Indo-Arabic numerals, but the symbol 'ϕ' to indicate the number zero.[47] The fact that we use the *same* symbol to indicate the number zero and empty places in the Indo-Arabic notation may have led to the often-repeated claim that the number zero is necessary for a place-value system. This claim is already refuted by the Babylonian place-value systems, but these still employ a mark for an empty place, either a space or a character. A more thorough study of place-value notations, however, reveals that even an empty-place marker is not necessary: It is possible to design place-value notations in which there are no empty places and every character has a nonzero value.[48]

Notational artifacts can also arise from the application of manipulations, Cardano's already mentioned introduction of the roots of negative numbers being

45 See Figure 5 for an example of a Babylonian base-60 numeral expression.

46 Further roles of '0' can be distinguished, see Schlimm and Skosnik (2011) for a discussion.

47 Cajori (1928a, 171–172).

48 Foster (1947).

the most famous example. Here, a term corresponding to '$\sqrt{-1}$' occurred as a subexpression when certain values were used in a general formula for the solution of polynomial equations. However, while negative numbers and roots of positive numbers were deemed unproblematic, the term expressing their combination was not considered to have an independent numerical meaning. Similar examples are Boole's use of expressions such as '$x + x$' in his symbolic logic, which he himself considered as 'uninterpretable' in logic and for which he was severely criticized by later logicians; this despite the fact that he made sure that these kinds of expressions would only appear within a computation, but never as the result. The expressions '$\frac{1}{0}$' and '$\frac{0}{0}$' look syntactically correct in our usual arithmetic, but because they do not have a meaningful interpretation, they are not allowed, while '$\frac{0}{1}$' is perfectly fine. In other words, we can consider the former as notational artifacts that are barred from being used in arithmetic.[49]

In addition to the somewhat general considerations discussed in this section, the relation between a notation and its intended subject matter also gives rise to more fundamental philosophical questions regarding the subject matter. We shall take these up again in Section 5.

3.2 Reading and Language

Many mathematical notations are introduced for an intended subject matter that can already be expressed in various languages. For example, it seems plausible that some number words existed before the introduction of written numeral systems, and certainly some Latin and English words played a logical role before the logical connectives were expressed symbolically. However, notations are not purely derivative of verbalizations, but they can also influence the language in which they are verbalized. Thus, we can ask: (a) How does reading influence a notation? And, (b) how does the notation influence reading?

Although we can copy and share written notations without expressing them in words, reading and verbalizing a notation makes it easier to use, communicate, and understand. Since languages are spoken in time, this requires the parsing of expressions in a linear order, for which there might not be an obvious way in the case of non-linear notations. To solve this problem, we frequently adopt reading conventions. For example, the formula

$$\sum_{i=0}^{n} i$$

[49] Notational artifacts thus share some commonalities with Lakatos' 'monsters', an observation that is worth further explorations (Lakatos, 1976).

is typically read as something like: 'The sum of the *i*s from *i* equal zero to *n*' or '… where *i* ranges from zero to *n*'. In this example we also notice how language can influence the choice of characters that are being used: The sum is expressed by the Greek letter 'Σ', which corresponds to the Latin 'S', the first letter of the word 'sum' (analogously, we use the Greek 'Π' (*pi*) to symbolize products). In fact, the technique of *mnemonics*, that is, the use of the first letter(s) of the name of the mathematical entity one intends to denote, is very popular and helps with memorizing the meaning of the symbol – albeit indirectly, through its verbalization. Examples abound, such as early symbols for addition and subtraction, 'p' and 'm' (plus and minus), and the common use of the variable '*t*' to represent time. Such mnemonics are not restricted to letters, but can also involve the use of symbols with already established meanings: for example, Hilbert used '&' for logical conjunction, appealing to the established use of the ampersand for 'and'.

At this point it is also useful to issue a warning: Not every plausible explanation for the choice of a character must indeed be the original motivation. Rather, such an explanation might well be given retrospectively, for easier memorization. For example, although one frequently finds the claim that the symbol '∨' for logical disjunction originates from the Latin *vel*, this does not seem to find support in the textual record.[50]

Exploiting prior verbalizations of the intended subject matter is not restricted to the shapes of individual characters, but it can also influence the structure of the respective notation. For example, the use of spacing to separate consecutive blocks of digits of long Indo-Arabic numerals was already mentioned above (Section 2.2.6). This partitioning into blocks of three digits appears very natural to English speakers, because it accords well with the verbal segmentation of number words into thousands, millions, and so on:

15143982721 vs. 15 143 982 721 vs. 151 4398 2721.

That the notational convention is indeed tied to the verbalization becomes obvious when taking other languages into consideration. For example, number words in Mandarin are segmented into ten-thousands, hundred millions, and so on. Accordingly, speakers of Mandarin typically separate a long digit into groups of four. Thus, they would find the third example above to be the more intuitive notation. A better match between the structures of a spoken language and a notation also has effects on the learning process. For example, because Mandarin number words are formed more regularly than

[50] Elkind and Zach (2023).

those of most European languages (and are also shorter), children who speak Mandarin typically learn the Indo-Arabic numerals faster than their European peers.[51]

In addition to the ease of readability in a spoken language, the partitioning of longer expressions also reduces the number of symbols that must be processed at the same time in order to read an expression. To determine how many objects one is presented with, empirical findings about the limitations of human perception mostly agree that we can immediately grasp the numerosity of up to four objects without counting (subitizing). Thus, to determine the value represented by a tally, such as '||||||||', all individual strokes have to be counted; but, in an expression in Roman numerals, such as 'VIII', the three occurrences of the same symbol are perceived at a glance. Accordingly, the segmentation of Indo-Arabic numerals into groups of three (or four) not only fits well with their verbalization in English (or Mandarin), but is also cognitively advantageous. (As this feature is relative to the cognitive resources of human users of a notation, it will be taken up again in Section 3.3)

Cases in which a notation influences the language are more rare, because some kind of verbalization is often in place before the adoption of a notation. However, sometimes such a verbalization might not cover all cases. Fibonacci, for example, when introducing the Indo-Arabic numerals to his readers in 1202, took the time to explain how they are systematically read, such that "you will be able to read a number, no matter how many figures"; his example is the 15-figure numeral $\overset{\frown}{678}\,\overset{\frown}{935}\,\overset{\frown}{784}\,\overset{\frown}{105}\,296$, which is to be read as "six hundred and seventy-eight thousand thousand thousand thousand, nine hundred thirty-five thousand thousand thousand, seven hundred and eighty-four thousand thousand, one hundred and five thousand, and two hundred and ninety-six."[52] Number words like 'million' were introduced in English only over a century later.

In addition, here are some more considerations in this direction, namely how the structure of operations (see Section 2.2.4) can interact with the ease of verbalizing algebraic expressions. The infix notation '5 + 7' might at first seem most convenient to us, because the order of the characters corresponds to the verbalization 'five plus seven.' However, the prefix and postfix notations can also be verbalized in a straightforward way: '+ 5 7' as 'the sum of 5 and 7,' and '5 7 +' as '5 and 7 added.' Indeed, in many everyday situations speaking of 'the sum of ...' might be the more natural formulation. When the expressions are nested, another issue arises that affects the ease of verbalization, namely grouping. Consider the following three cases:

[51] Miller et al. (2005).
[52] Sigler (2002, 20).

Notation	Verbalization
$3 \times (5 + 7)$	Three times five plus seven.
$\times\ 3 + 5\ 7$	The product of three with the sum of five and seven.
$5\ 7 + 3\ \times$	Five and seven added and with three multiplied.

Here, the first verbalization is more concise, but it is ambiguous with regard to the order in which the operations are to be carried out. To remove this ambiguity we usually add a pause between 'times' and 'five plus seven,' saying 'three times – five plus seven.' Pauses like this, however, appear to be more of an artifact of trying to read the expression from left to right than a natural way of speaking. In fact, it could well be that the verbalization 'five plus seven' became common only *in response* to the practice of writing arithmetical expressions in a particular way. If this were the case, a justification of the order of operations in our algebraic notation with the naturalness of verbalization would obviously be circular. As the verbalization of the prefix expression does not require any artificial pauses, it is possibly clearer and easier to understand. However, with more levels of nesting any form of verbal expression will quickly become too difficult to understand. For the time being, some of the claims made in this paragraph remain speculative, and more linguistic, historical, and empirical research is necessary to study the interrelations between notations and language.

Opportunities for coining new verbalizations occur when new mathematical notions are introduced. A clear-cut case in which the language was influenced by a choice of representation has been documented by Carter (2010). In her case study of a proof in free probability theory, she found that the mathematicians in question introduced a graphical notation for the representation of certain permutations in which some lines crossed each other. This graphical property led to the terminology of 'crossing' pairs (as well as 'neighboring' pairs and 'removing' a pair from the diagram), even though the graphical notation did not appear at all in the published paper and the definitions were introduced in purely algebraic terms.[53]

3.3 Users and Their Cognitive Resources

To be employed in a meaningful way, a notation has to be learned and understood. These are complex processes that depend in part on the characters and structure of the notation and in part on the users' cognitive resources and prior experience. Thus, discussions of the *users* of notational systems rely to a

[53] Carter (2010, 11).

considerable extent on results from research in psychology and cognitive science. In addition, since users live in a society at a specific time, sociological, cultural, and historical considerations can also come into play when evaluating notations.

3.3.1 Learning

To appreciate the effort involved in learning a new notation, a brief sketch of how children learn to understand and use the Indo-Arabic notation for numbers, which has been studied extensively by developmental psychologists, is revealing in many ways.[54] Typically, a child begins by learning a sequence of number words, say 'one, two, three, …' in English. At this point, no particular meanings are yet associated with the sounds, it is simply a fixed sequence, such as 'eeny, meeny, miny, moe'. Then, the child learns to repeat the sequence while pointing at individual objects of a certain kind, thereby creating a one-to-one correlation between the number words and the objects. The next step is to associate the last used word with the quantity of the counted objects. Developmentally, this step is learned in different subsequent stages, one for each number word from 'one' to 'four', after which the child has typically mastered the *cardinality principle* for all number words that it knows. Furthermore, to apply the basic arithmetical operations, one has to correlate the number words to numerals and to learn addition and multiplication tables by heart, or invent shortcuts to reconstruct them using a counting-on procedure. After learning the basic written arithmetic operations for single-digit numerals, these are extended to multidigit numerals, where the order in which the columns have to be processed, the handling of empty places, and the tracking of carries and borrows pose additional difficulties. Mistakes that are systematically made during this learning phase often reveal the lack of a thorough understanding of the place-value structure of the notation.[55]

What the preceding account shows is that the learning of both the notation and the subject matter, namely cardinal numbers and basic arithmetic, goes hand in hand and that the structure of the numeral system is learned in part by performing written operations with it.

3.3.2 Understanding

We have seen in the case of learning basic arithmetic that verbalization plays a crucial role and we have discussed how this is connected to various features of a notation in Section 3.2. However, we do not only seek to verbalize a notation,

---

[54] See Pantsar (2024) for an overview and further discussion.

[55] See Schlimm (2018) for an overview and further references.

but also to understand it. This involves not only being able to name the expressions, but also knowing how the basic symbols relate to their referents, how the structure of the notation contributes to the meaning of complex expressions, and how to correctly manipulate the expressions.

In particular, understanding the *structure* of expressions is often much more difficult than being able to name expressions and basic symbols. For example, while children at a certain stage of their development might be able to name '18' as 'eighteen', they can still lack the understanding that the '1' stands for ten and the '8' stands for eight.[56] For them, asking what the '1' means in '18' is analogous to asking what the letter 't' means in the word 'ten'. Thus, by learning the Indo-Arabic notation, prior conceptions of numbers are refined: The characterization of numbers in terms of powers of a base emerges, as does the conviction that every number, no matter how large, has a canonical representation or name – note that this is not the case for verbal numeral systems, which are all limited.

Another behavioral pattern that reveals a lack of understanding of the structure of a notation is the common mistake of beginners of calculus to cancel out the '*d*' in '$\frac{dx}{dy}$', as they would do if this was an algebraic expression.[57]

Once we are familiar with a particular notation these matters all appear to us as being straightforward, and we wonder how somebody could have difficulties with them. However, we thereby frequently forget how long and tedious the learning process was and how many difficulties we had with it ourselves. This makes it quite difficult to imagine how it was when we did not understand the notation. Acknowledging these difficulties is particularly important for mathematics educators.

3.3.3 Novices and Experts

The discussion of some of the difficulties involved in learning a new notation illustrates that there is often a wide gap between novices and experts when it comes to learning, understanding, and using a mathematical notation. More specifically, there are features of notations that can make them easier to learn but more cumbersome to be used by experts, and vice versa. For example, the numerical value represented by small Roman numerals, for example, 'III', can be accessed in three different ways: first, by counting the occurrences of 'I' in the expression; second, by immediately recognizing that there are three 'I's in the expression (subitizing); and, third, by considering 'III' as a single, complex symbol, whose meaning has to be memorized. These different paths available

56 Schlimm (2018, 204–207).

57 Thanks to Jessica Carter for sharing this example.

in the Roman numeral system can be exploited by users with different levels of expertise, thus making the system generally more accessible. In contrast, the only way to access the meaning of the Indo-Arabic numeral '3' is to memorize it. But here the information is represented by a single symbol, rather than with three, which is advantageous for other tasks. Thus, when discussing the use of a notation it is crucial to keep in mind who it was designed for and who is using it.

3.3.4 Thinking in Symbols

After learning and understanding a notational system, we are in a position to employ it for specific tasks, a process we might be inclined to call 'thinking *with* symbols' and which is discussed in Section 3.4. From the perspective of extended cognition, a popular position in the philosophy of mind, such uses of notations are indeed also cognitive tasks that interact with the users' internal cognitive resources, such as memory, attention span, and so on. In addition, I agree with Tolchinsky that learning and understanding a notation amounts to a cognitive 'transformation',[58] which also changes our internal mental representations. More recently, this process has been characterized as "the integration of cognitive tools into our cognitive systems as a process of enculturation."[59] In other words, we also think *in* symbols, which justifies the two-way arrow between notations and users shown in Figure 2.

The best evidence for the internalization of notations comes from the most-studied notational system, namely the Indo-Arabic numerals. Various empirical results about size comparisons and mental calculations can be explained best as representational effects that indicate that the mental processes are carried out in a notation and not on some other kind of homogeneous internal representation, such as an analog magnitude system or a mental number line. For example, when shown one of these two pairs of numerals and asked which of the numerals represents a greater number,

42 <?> 57 47 <?> 62

people tend to give faster and more accurate responses when they are shown the first pair rather than the second, despite the fact that the difference (or distance) between 47 and 62 is the same as that between 42 and 57. This phenomenon is called the "unit-decade compatibility effect."[60] The difference in reaction times

[58] Tolchinsky (2003, xix).
[59] Menary and Gillett (2022, 363).
[60] Nuerk et al. (2001).

cannot be explained by the relevant size of the represented numbers. Instead, in the first case, both the units and the tens of the numeral '42' are less than those of '57', but in '47' the tens are less, but the units are more than in '62'. In other words, the mental comparison between the values relies on distinguishing between units and tens, which is a property of the numerals, but not of the numbers – after all, abstract numbers are not composed of digits. Other results that support this conclusion have been found in many other experiments involving transcoding tasks and mental arithmetic.[61]

Empirical results such as those just mentioned led cognitive scientists to include the structure of the Indo-Arabic numerals into their models of mental representations of numbers. While Dehaene's 1992 triple-code representation of numbers explicitly included only the visual representation of the Indo-Arabic numerals in addition to a verbal representation and the analog magnitude system,[62] Nuerk and his colleagues have explicitly added a "structural representation of the symbolic number system (place-value representation)" into their more recent model of our internal representations.[63] Extensive research in neuroscience supports this claim: The structural representation is learned and then internalized. Accordingly, users who grew up knowing only Roman numerals presumably would also have a different internal representation of numbers.

3.3.5 Values

A rarely addressed issue, which also depends on the users of a notation, is the values associated with a notation that are independent of its practical uses.[64] For example, the medieval Arabic mathematician Al-Uqlīdisī remarks that the decimal place-value system was generally frowned upon because it was typically used on a dust abacus, which "is indeed ugly to see in the hands of the scribe" and "which is rather unbecoming from the point of view of many people." To save the scribe from "the misinterpretation of the populace" he suggests to replace the characters and use them with ink and paper.[65] The fact that the Indo-Arabic numerals were adopted fairly late by Western European merchants and bankers, despite their use in calendrical and astronomical calculations, is explained by Durham not by any practical advantages, but with reference to Renaissance culture and education, which ultimately led to the

---

61 See Nuerk et al. (2015) for an overview.

62 Dehaene (1992, 31).

63 Nuerk et al. (2015).

64 I thank Roi Wagner for sharing an unpublished draft where some of the observations and the references that follow are discussed.

65 Saidan (1978, 35–36, 310).

Roman numerals being discredited.[66] Regarding the general adoption of the Indo-Arabic numerals, Chrisomalis adds material and social factors, such as the "advent of widespread literacy and the printing press, and the integration of local economies and social institutions into global systems."[67] Other values, such as nationalist sentiments can also influence the evaluation of notational systems, for example, in the famous dispute between Newton and Leibniz on the origin of the calculus and the adoption of Leibnizian methods in England. Nationalistic and ideological perspectives on mathematics can also be found in the nineteenth and twentieth centuries, although they seem to have been directed more against groups of mathematicians or mathematical styles, rather than particular notation systems.[68] Nevertheless, when it comes to the adoption of a notation, prestige, status, national pride, and other values that are associated with a particular system should not be neglected.

3.4 Tasks and Algorithms

3.4.1 Representational Tasks

By addressing the question 'What are notations used for?' we shift our attention to the particular tasks for which notations are employed. Some tasks concern all notations, such as learning and understanding a notation; we have already discussed the task of *reading*, in relation to their users (Section 3.3), and we shall look at the *writing* of notations in relation to their materiality in Section 3.5. Other tasks that notations are commonly used for include those typical for external representations, such as *encoding information* about the intended subject matter in such a way that it can be recorded and communicated to others.[69] That the way information is stored affects its retrieval should be obvious. Just imagine a library in which the books are not ordered by topic and author's last name, but by title, or by year of publication, or by the color of the cover, or by the size of the book. This would require very different (and possibly quite inefficient) algorithms for finding a particular book, although it could also prove to be quite effective for certain tasks (e.g., finding the smallest book).

The ease and availability of information is closely linked to how the primitives of the intended subject matter are mapped to notational elements and to the distinction between *explicit* and *implicit* representations. At first sight, these notions might seem straightforward as concerning the distinction between

66 Durham (1992).
67 Chrisomalis (2020, 121–122).
68 See, for example, Siegmund-Schultze (1991).
69 See also Kirsh (2010) for a general discussion of the uses of external representations.

notational elements that one can *see* immediately and those one cannot, but the matter is more subtle. After all, something external always has to trigger the interpretation of an expression, and one always has to know something (internal) to interpret it. Kirsh (1990) convincingly criticized a naive characterization of explicitness and proposed to regard it from a computational perspective on the usability of information, as the interplay "between the procedures available to the agent and the forms the content is encoded in."[70] Let us look at some simple examples of common algebraic expressions for multiplication and exponentiation:

$$2 \cdot x \qquad 2x \qquad 2^{x} \qquad 2^{x} \qquad \exp(2, x).$$

These expressions pose no difficulties for a mathematical reader, but they differ with respect to which notational elements indicate the operation and what a user has to know in order to understand them. If the primitive (i.e., the operation) is represented by a specific string of characters, such as '·' and 'exp', it can easily be located. Nevertheless, there are differences even in this case: that the dot stands for multiplication has to be memorized, but the meaning of 'exp' is already hinted at by the term itself, since it is a mnemonic for 'exponentiation'; moreover, 'exp' is located at one of the endpoints of the expression, which are perceptually more salient. In the cases of '$2x$' and '2^{x}' there is no specific character that stands for the operation, but it is represented by the arrangement of characters. In '$2x$', the operation of multiplication is indicated simply by the juxtaposition of the characters; juxtaposition is used in all examples to form the strings, but in '$2x$' it also refers to a primitive of the intended subject matter. This has to be inferred by the reader, who has to learn that the juxtaposition of a numeral and a variable stands for multiplication. The operation in '2^{x}' can be inferred by the raised 'x', which is further emphasized by the use of a smaller font for the variable in '2^{x}'. In practice, the ease of reading these expressions depends on the time to access and process their notational elements. According to Kirsh, this can lead to situations in which the structural immediacy and the process immediacy of information do not line up, as the latter depends on "individual capacities for memory, learning, and other cognitive skills."[71]

In general, the more a notation relies on characters, the easier it is to learn, because the learner can exploit more visible cues. However, the more such cues need to be accessed and processed, the longer it generally takes to interpret and use the notation; then again, less reliance on such cues can make a notation more immediate and faster to process for an expert.

---

[70] Kirsh (1990, 345).
[71] Kirsh (2003, 480).

3.4.2 Operational Tasks

In addition to the tasks of reading, writing, and encoding information, which apply to most representational systems, a particular notation is usually also employed for very specific tasks. For example, numerals are not only used to represent a quantity (e.g., the population of a country) or to simply provide unique names for a sequence of objects (e.g., in street addresses), but also to calculate with them and thereby to gain insights into the relations between numbers, the intended subject matter of arithmetic. Algebraic equations are often transformed into other equations, so that we can learn something about the abstract relationships that they express. Expressions for functions are expanded, and expressions for their derivatives and integrals are obtained. Logical inferences are applied to formulas to form proofs, which tell us how premises are linked to a conclusion. These are just a handful of examples that illustrate the crucial role of the operative component of mathematical notations.

The accomplishment of each individual task that a notation is employed for depends in part on the notational elements themselves and the particular algorithm that is employed, but in part also on other aspects of a notation, such as the resources that are provided by the user and the material basis of the notation. This makes the analysis of how suited a notation is for a particular task more difficult than one might expect.

A very influential approach to assess representations with regard to specific tasks was proposed by Larkin and Simon (1987). After introducing the distinction between *informational equivalence* and *computational equivalence* of representations, they went on to investigate the computational differences between external representations, such as a diagram illustrating several weights and pulleys and a sentential representation with the same informational content. In particular, they abstracted from the specific nature of the representations by identifying certain operations that can be performed quickly on the respective representations and used these to formulate algorithms for specific tasks. The efficiency of these algorithms was then used as a proxy for the computational efficiency of the representation.[72]

A more refined analysis of distributed cognitive tasks involving mathematical notations was given by Zhang and Norman (1995), who distinguish between the contribution of external representations, whose informational content can be accessed through perception, and internal representations, whose information has to be retrieved from (long-term or short-term) memory. Empirical findings about the limitations of human cognition mostly agree that we can

---

[72] See Waszek (2024) for a discussion of Larkin and Simon's approach.

keep seven plus or minus two elements in our working memory. Notational systems that demand more than these would put an excessive strain on our cognitive resources. In addition to the retrieval of information, the perceptual and mental processes must also be coordinated, which is done by a central control, which also "executes arithmetic procedures, allocates attentional resources, and performs other processes that are necessary for the completion of the task."[73] Consider, for example, the complexity of a task that many are still quite familiar with, namely adding several numerals using paper and pencil. To accomplish this, one has to learn the values of the individual digits and a certain algorithm, then process the numerals column-wise, starting from the units, recall the addition table for each individual single-digit addition, write the unit value of the result in the appropriate position and remember the value of the tens to carry over to the next column on the left. Thus, despite the fact that this is an algorithm performed on written numerals, it requires some information to be stored in long-term memory (symbol values, algorithm, addition facts) and other in short-term memory (position of focus of attention, intermediate results, carries). Due to the load on working memory, Zhang and Norman assert that "the more information needs to be retrieved from internal representations, the harder the task."[74] Other algorithms, however, might externalize the intermediate sums and thereby require less information to be kept in short-term memory, at the cost of having to write more symbols. This illustrates again that the assessment of notations in terms of operational tasks does not only depend on the structure of the notation, but is also very sensitive to the particular algorithms employed.

3.5 Materiality and Writing

The shapes of the characters and the structure of a mathematical notation depend in part on how the expressions are produced. In the case of written notations this means where and how they are written.

While we can imagine a particular inscription on any kind of surface, the choice of a particular writing surface, such as paper, parchment, sand, clay, or stone, affects the design and use of a notation. For example, the form of the writing material can influence the layout of the writing, and the cost of the writing material can determine the content that is deemed worthy of recording. The writing material also restricts what utensils can be used for the writing, which affects the shape, size, or colors of the characters. For example, ancient Babylonian inscriptions were made with a reed stylus on clay tablets, which

[73] Zhang and Norman (1995, 290).

[74] Zhang and Norman (1995, 287).

restricts the characters to combinations of a few simple shapes. Similarly, we can expect a different notational design depending on whether it is intended to be written by hand with a pen, or with a typewriter. The ease of writing by hand is often used by authors to argue in favor of their own choice of characters. For example, one of Jevons' reasons for preferring to express the negation of 'A' with a lowercase 'a' instead of adding a prime, 'A'', is that "it is written with one pen-stroke less, which in the long run is a matter of importance."[75] When comparing his own choice of using the character '$-\!\!<$' instead of Schröder's '$\leqq$' for logical consequence, Peirce comments that the latter "cannot be written rapidly enough."[76] He further adds the advantages of his character both for printing and handwriting: "It is easily made in the composing room from a dash followed by <, and in its cursive form is struck off in two rapid strokes, thus ≺."[77]

The advent of printing, in particular with movable types, added another layer of constraints to the production of writing. Instead of inventing new characters, which would require the production of new types, it was much more convenient to combine readily available types, such as Peirce's '$-\!\!<$', or to rotate already existing types (leading to cognate characters, see Section 2.1.2).[78] Characters that would require extra vertical space would also make the production more expensive, which is why Peano recommended to write fractions in a single line, that is, as 'a/b' instead of '$\dfrac{a}{b}$'.[79] In contemporary typesetting, the size of the letters is often reduced to avoid extra spacing between lines, as in '$\tfrac{a}{b}$'. Another effect of printing is that the use of color has decreased, due to the added costs. In the case of texts in electronic format, however, adding color no longer incurs any additional costs and we notice the return of the colored texts on our screens.

The material basis of notations can also affect the design of algorithms for manipulating expressions. For example, marks on a dust abacus can easily be erased and replaced by others without leaving a trace, whereas this is not possible when calculations are performed with ink on paper. Here, superfluous marks must be crossed out, so that the individual steps of a calculation remain visible; this requires more space, but also makes it possible to retrace the individual steps.

[75] Jevons (1896, xiv–xvi).
[76] Peirce (1870, 2).
[77] Peirce (1897, 187–188).
[78] See also the characters used by Leibniz, shown on p. 4.
[79] See Schlimm (2021, 112–113) for a discussion of Peano's concerns regarding printing costs and typographical convenience.

3.6 Notational Traditions

By the time one introduces a new notation one typically has already learned to use other notations, so that these affect the design of the new notation. This influence can extend to the choice of characters and the structure of the expressions, but it can also go so far as including an earlier notation in the new design, leading to nested notations (see Section 2.2.5).

The deliberate use of characters from other notations can have several reasons. First, it could be just a matter of employing a familiar notation for a related notion. For example, a raised '2' can be used to indicate the twofold application of an operation, even if this operation is not multiplication, for which the superscripts were originally used. Second, since learning new symbols, structural arrangements, or methods of grouping is typically difficult, appealing to familiar principles also increases the likelihood of acceptance of a new notation. Finally, using already established notational elements can be intended to express some relation of affinity between the two notational systems. Boole, for example, used the characters '+' and '×' for logical disjunction and conjunction to highlight the structural similarity of the underlying laws, and so his readers felt quite familiar with the new notation. Moreover, later logicians who worked in the algebra of logic tradition that Boole started, such as Schröder, also tended to employ the characters that he used. Tracing such notational traditions can yield information about the authors' conceptions of the intended subject matter, an issue that we will take up again in Section 5.1.1.

4 The Design of Mathematical Notations

Many discussions of notations revolve around the questions of what makes a notation good or whether one notation is better than another. Designing and assessing notations seem to be two sides of the same coin. After all, when we design a notation we want it to be a good notation, and by assessing a notation we find out whether it is good or not. However, there is also an asymmetry: When designing a notation, we often have some particular users and tasks in mind, but when assessing a notation, more general considerations can come into play. Specifically, we might want to assess a versatile notation without knowing for which purpose it was originally designed. The various aspects of notations introduced in Section 3 provide us with an overview of the considerations that can be brought to bear in the assessment of a notation. Moreover, rather than assessing a notation individually it is often more fruitful to compare two notations, as this allows us to identify those features of the notations that make a difference.

While one might think that some notations are better than others *tout court* – and indeed one can frequently read claims that one notation is superior to another – we must keep in mind that the goodness of a notation is *relative* to specific tasks and users. This was already illustrated with the example of keeping track of beverage orders in the Introduction (Section 1.3.4). An overall assessment can then only be obtained by weighing the relevance of these different tasks. This, of course, bears the risk of emphasizing those tasks in which one's favorite notation does better, without attempting to further justify this choice. Instead, a more nuanced and less subjective analysis can often be given by discussing the trade-offs between different notations without insisting on providing an overall judgment.

When it comes to general design criteria, one might at first think of *simplicity* (or economy). However, without further specification this is not really helpful, as the idea that a good notation should be simple can be cashed out in various ways: for example, in terms of syntax, that expressions should be concise; in terms of semantics, that we should represent only fundamental notions as primitive; and in pragmatic terms, that the notation should be easy to use. Given that usability typically includes reading, writing, and other tasks that the notation can be employed for, it should not come as a surprise that the aim of devising a simple notation can lead to different, and possibly conflicting, recommendations about what the notation should look like. Thus, again, we should keep in mind that the design choices for a particular notation are generally based on trade-offs and compromises.

4.1 Expression Length and Number of Symbols

4.1.1 Length of Expressions

The conciseness or terseness of expressions has been one of the most frequently mentioned aims in the design of notations for at least the past two centuries: It is listed as one of the main desiderata for a notation in Babbage's 1830 entry on 'Notation' in the *Edinburgh Encyclopedia*:

> The great object of all notation is to convey to the mind, as speedily as possible, a complete idea of operations which are to be, or have been, executed; since every thing is to be exhibited to the eye, the more compact and condensed the symbols are, the more readily they will be caught, as it were, at a glance.[80]

If an expression is short, Babbage argues, it can be read faster and more information can be taken in at the same time. That this contributes to achieving

[80] Babbage (1830, 412); see also Dutz and Schlimm (2021).

a better overview is echoed in the twentieth century on the first pages of Whitehead and Russell's *Principia Mathematica* (1910): "The terseness of the symbolism enables a whole proposition to be represented to the eyesight as one whole, or at most in two or three parts divided where the natural breaks, represented in the symbolism, occur."[81]

While the conciseness of expressions seems to be an uncontroversial design goal, its implementation is not always straightforward. For example, Roman numerals are, on average, about 2.6 times longer than the corresponding Indo-Arabic numerals, but some are in fact shorter (e.g., 'M' vs. '1000'). Moreover, instead of simply averaging the lengths of a certain range of expressions, it could be more appropriate to also take into account the frequency in which expressions are actually used in a particular practice. A simple search on the Internet for the number of occurrences of the expressions '999' and '1000' reveals that the latter occurs almost ten times as often. Thus, having a shorter expression for it could in fact reduce the overall lengths of actually used numerals. Frege also appealed to the frequency in actual usage to argue for his choice of primitives in logic.[82] One lesson to be learned here is the crucial importance that particular uses can play in an overall assessment of a notation, even if we just consider the length of expressions.

4.1.2 Number of Basic Symbols

Conciseness of expressions alone cannot be the sole criterion for the goodness of a notation. Otherwise, we would always prefer notations in which most expressions consist of a single symbol, which, in turn, would yield a substantial increase in the number of basic symbols of the notation. This points at a trade-off between the conciseness of expressions and the number of basic symbols to be used, both of which can affect any of the aspects of a notation discussed in Section 3, including the number of primitive notions of the intended subject matter that can be represented, the amount of information (symbols, formation rules, etc.) that has to be memorized, and the readability of expressions.

Minimizing the number of basic symbols may be hailed as a theoretical achievement (such as Sheffer's reduction of propositional logic to a single connective), but it typically also increases the length of expressions (such as representing logical formulas using only the Sheffer stroke, or representing numbers by tallies). Therefore, this is often not taken to be the most decisive criterion in notational design. Instead, some sort of balance between the number of basic symbols and the length of expressions is usually sought after.

[81] Whitehead and Russell (1910, 3).
[82] See Schlimm (2018, 71).

4.2 Users and Intended Subject Matter

4.2.1 Learning and Proficiency

For human users, understanding a notation is crucial. After all, in order to be used, a notational system must be understood. This involves knowing the meaning of the symbols, the implicit conventions, and how the structure of an expression contributes to its meaning. Learning these aspects of a notation involves getting acquainted with new symbols and expressions as well as algorithms for their manipulations. Most of this information has to be memorized, and carrying out the manipulations frequently puts additional load on our short-term memory. The underlying mechanisms, studied in developmental psychology and cognitive science, and the perceptual and cognitive resources needed for becoming proficient with a notational system can be an important factor in its assessment.

The ease of learning a notation can also make a difference in the case of diagrammatic notations. Consider, for example, the two expressions for knots shown in Figure 3. Presumably, they differ only in the way they represent which strands pass above another in the crossings. I assume that most readers will have enough familiarity with such representations to correctly interpret Figure 3(a), but are perhaps confused about the diagram in Figure 3(b). Accordingly, we might be tempted to consider the left notation to be more 'natural'. However, what we see at a crossing of the form ' ⤫ ' are really three separate line segments and to interpret two of them as being connected and passing under the other has to be learned. Similarly, the meaning of the dots has to be learned, but that is not too difficult either. As Alexander explains his notation: "The convention will be to place the dots in such a manner that an insect crawling in the positive sense along the 'lower' branch through a crossing point would always have the two dotted corners on its left."[83] We could also imagine the two dots as plier tips that grasp the strand between them and pull it up. Considering the

(a) Common notation.

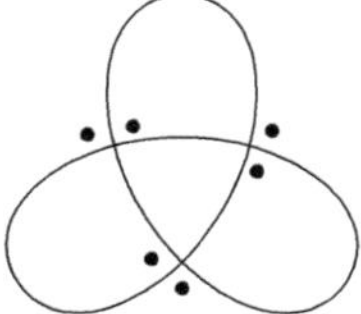

(b) Alexander's dot notation.

Figure 3 Two notations for the trefoil knot.

[83] Alexander (1928, 277).

material production of these figures, either by hand or in printing, Alexander's notation might well be more convenient and it might also be read more reliably, because the dots are easier to recognize than the missing piece of curved line. Thus, we notice again how the consideration of various aspects of a notation complicates an unambiguous assessment.

If one is only interested in how a notation is employed by expert users, then all considerations and difficulties of learning the notation can be neglected. This, however, complicates the analysis of notations further, because it is difficult to know what exactly experts bring to the table when using a notation (see the problem of familiarity in the study of notations, Section 1.3.2). For this reason, to level the playing field, psychological experiments on the use of notations are often based on the artificial symbol learning paradigm, where a novel notation is first learned and then used. If notations are intended to be processed by computers, then the tasks of learning and understanding are replaced by parsing the expressions and translating them into some data structure.

4.2.2 Informational Equivalence and Choice of Primitives

To achieve a fair comparison between different systems of representation, Larkin and Simon suggested to compare only representations that are informationally equivalent.[84] However, given that a subject matter can be carved up into different primitives (see Section 3.1.1), we should really distinguish between determining the primitives of a subject matter and choosing a notation for those primitives. The latter, of course, depends on the former, but the questions of *what* to represent and *how* to represent it should be kept separate in an analysis of notations. (But this is not always easy: For example, in the case of the Sheffer stroke at the end of Section 4.1.2, we should really have said that the reduction of basic symbols was achieved through a reduction of the number of primitives that were represented; the change of notation was a consequence of a change of subject matter.) The reason for the keeping apart of subject matter and notation is that some properties of a notation can depend to a large extent on the choice of primitives, regardless of other design choices. For example, the average length of expressions in a notation for propositional logic that represents only negation and implication will certainly be longer than a notation that also represents additional connectives (such as conjunction, disjunction, and bi-implication), because the latter have to be expressed in terms of the former. A general criticism of Frege's *Begriffsschrift* notation for logic in terms of the length of its expressions, as was put forward by his

[84] Larkin and Simon (1987). See also Section 3.4.2.

colleague Schröder, is therefore independent of Frege's choice of characters and their arrangements, and could easily be responded to by adding symbols for additional logical primitives.[85]

The notion of informational equivalence is indeed often more thorny than it might at first seem. For example, consider again the two notations for knots shown in Figure 3. I discussed them in the previous section only in relation to how they represent the location of strands at a crossing, but upon further reflection we notice that the two notations also differ in what they represent: On the one hand, Alexander's instructions on how to read the dots referred to a specific direction in which the insect would crawl on the branches. Thus, the dot notation also codifies a sense, or direction, of the curve, which the other notation does not. In short, the two notations do not carry exactly the same information. And, in fact, Alexander and Briggs introduce the dot notation as a "better notation for our present purposes," because they also refer to the dots in the mathematical reasoning itself by distinguishing between two different kinds of incident relation between a point and a region, namely "incident *with*, or *without a dot*."[86] On the other hand, in the notation shown in Figure 3(a), the closed curve clearly appears as being separated into three different arcs. Imagining these components as being colored in different ways yields the notion of a colored (or labeled) knot diagram, which leads to the notion of tricolorability of knot diagrams, which in turn is a knot invariant and is used to prove the existence of different knot types. Of course, these notions can also be defined in terms of Alexander's dot notation, but in a less direct and visibly compelling way. Thus, the two notations differ with regard to both their representational and their operational aspects.

4.2.3 Symbol Shapes and Their Meanings

From the perspective of a notation as merely representational, the particular shapes of the characters are in principle arbitrary, which underlies Peirce's notion of a symbol (see Section 3.1.2). In practice, however, notations are always introduced and used in a context (see Section 3) and the shapes of characters can be motivated, for example, by employing previously used characters, by their function within an expression (e.g., to combine an operation with its scope or to attract the reader's attention), or by external factors, such as printing costs or the availability of the typesetter. Certain shapes can also contribute to the usability of a notation for human users by being easier to read and write, and by facilitating memorizing their intended meanings.

---

85 For a detailed analysis and discussion of Frege's *Begriffsschrift* notation, see Schlimm (2018).

86 Alexander and Briggs (1926, 570).

To facilitate the association between a character and its meaning, various strategies can be pursued. If a verbalization already exists, the symbol can relate to the word that expresses the meaning (mnemonics; see Section 3.2). The meanings can also be indicated in relation to a cognate symbol, for example when using '⊥' for the negation of '⊤', or Carnap's use of 'D' for the domain of a binary relation and the inverted symbol 'ᗡ' for its range.[87] In addition, the shape of the character can be chosen to indicate the meaning through some sort of resemblance (iconicity; see Section 3.1.2). For example, the union of two sets is commonly represented by '∪', which resembles a cup in which the contents of the two sets can be collected; incidentally, it is also cognate to '∩', which is commonly used for the intersection of sets. Properties of a character can also allude to properties of what is denoted. For example, a symmetric character can indicate the commutativity of the represented operation, and, in fact, empirical studies have found the cognitive effectiveness of such a connection.[88]

Characters can also be selected intentionally to highlight certain analogies between different notational systems. For example, as we have already seen in the discussion of notational traditions (Section 3.6), Boole deliberately used the familiar arithmetical symbols '+', '−', and '×', for logical connectives, to emphasize the analogy between the laws of arithmetic and logic. This practice also invites the transfer of reasoning from a familiar domain to an unfamiliar one, which is advantageous if the reasoning is indeed correct, but can also lead to errors in the case that the transfer is invalid. In logic, for example, conjunction and disjunction are distributive in both directions, while in arithmetic multiplication distributes over addition, while not the other way around. To hint at the analogy without using exactly the same symbol, later logicians used slight modifications of the arithmetical symbols (see Section 5.1.1).

The practice of using the same symbol with different meanings is common in computer science. In the context of computer programming languages, for example, the practice of denoting functions of different types by the same characters is called 'operator overloading' and is used mainly for the convenience of the users. If the same code is used in the definitions of such operators, one speaks of 'polymorphism,' which has the advantage of reusing the same code in different circumstances, thereby reducing the possibilities of mistakes. These examples stand in contrast to the desideratum that each character should have a clear, determinate, and unique meaning. Nevertheless, this property of *univocity* is frequently mentioned, for example by Frege, as a requirement for notational systems. Of course, if '+' could mean both addition and subtraction

[87] Carnap (1929, 44).
[88] Wege et al. (2020).

within the same arithmetical system, it is hard to conceive how this ambiguous notation would be of much use. As usual, however, things are often more subtle in actual practice, where practical considerations often override philosophical concerns.

4.2.4 Syntactic and Semantic Alignment

The view that a good notation exhibits a systematic connection between notational elements and intended subject matter is not limited to the characters, but extends also to sets of characters and their arrangements in expressions. Ubiquitous in the design of notation is what we might call the 'similarity principle': *Cognate symbols should reflect similarities in meaning*. In other words, syntactic similarities (differences) should reflect semantic similarities (differences). We recognize applications of this principle in all our common notational systems: symbols for grouping have the same shapes, we use letters for variables with different fonts to represent different sorts, and operation symbols are frequently cognate.

A second general principle for the design of a notation concerns the structural arrangement of characters: *What belongs together should also appear together.* According to this 'togetherness principle,' elements of an expression should be grouped together according to their semantic reference, which makes it easier to parse an expression at a higher level of abstraction. For example, the lower and upper bounds of an integral are commonly shown close together, as in $\int_0^\infty \frac{x^2+x}{3}\,dx$. This allows us to identify the expression as an integral with its bounds and then to shift our attention to the formula itself. Alternatively, we could also think of a notation in which the bounds appear at the beginning and end of the expressions, as in: $\int_0 \frac{x^2+x}{3}\,dx \int^\infty$. Here, however, the values of the bounds are less convenient to parse, because the eye has to move from the beginning to the end of the expression. The use of variable-length symbols, such as the fraction bar (vinculum), also helps the eye to perceive the numerator and denominator as individual units. Being able to quickly grasp an entire expression is indeed an advantage of a notation that is frequently mentioned (see the quotations by Babbage, and Whitehead and Russell at the beginning of Section 4.1.1).

The importance of the togetherness principle has also been validated empirically by research in cognitive science. In a series of experiments, Landy and Goldstone have shown that students intuitively write characters closer together if they are semantically connected and, conversely, are more likely to interpret syntactic closeness also as semantically relevant. For example, despite the fact that multiplication binds stronger than addition, the expression '$5 \times 3+2$' is often interpreted erroneously as '$5 \times (3 + 2)$' instead of '$(5 \times 3) + 2$' because of the different spacing around the operators.[89]

4.2.5 Complex Symbols

In addition to making it easier to parse an expression, the practice of grouping symbols together that are semantically related can also have the effect that such a group can be treated as a single *complex symbol*. In the literature on the psychology of expert reasoning, such meaningful units formed from collections of simpler elements are called 'chunks.'[90] Through chunking, for example, the numerator and the denominator of a fraction that are separated by a horizontal line, as in $\frac{x^2+x}{3}$, can be seen and treated as two units. Thus, to form the reciprocal fraction, $\frac{3}{x^2+x}$, we can simply switch the entire subexpressions as if they were individual symbols. In fact, when solving arithmetical equations we often treat a sequence of digits as a single numeral, namely as a complex symbol, to be operated on, as in the rule of 'adding on both sides of an equation.'

Another striking example of how a notation lends itself to the formation of complex symbols is Frege's *Begriffsschrift* notation for logic, in which the logical connectives and the non-logical symbols are spatially separated within an expression, whereas they appear mixed together in the common linear logical notation. Compare, for example, the following two formulas, where the negation of 'X' is expressed in common notation by '$\neg X$' and in Frege's notation by '─┬─X', and where 'X' implies 'Y' is expressed by '$X \rightarrow Y$' and '─┬─Y └─X', respectively:

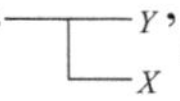

─┬──┬─┬─ B
  └─── A

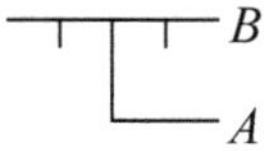

$\neg(A \rightarrow \neg B)$

We notice that the logical symbols appear as a single group in Frege's notation: we can easily draw a straight line separating the logical symbols from the non-logical ones, that is, 'A' and 'B'. After realizing that the preceding formulas are logically equivalent to conjunction, we can identify '─┬──┬─┬─' as a single complex symbol denoting logical conjunction. In the formula on the right, the negation and implication symbols ('$\neg$' and '$\rightarrow$') are interrupted by a parenthesis and a non-logical symbol 'A', which makes it more difficult to treat the pattern of logical symbols as a single entity.[91] The presence of complex symbols

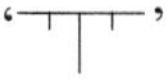

89 See Landy et al. (2014) for an overview of these results.

90 See Miller (1956) and Chase and Simon (1973).

91 For a discussion of complex symbols in Frege's *Begriffsschrift*, see Schlimm (2018).

in a notation allows for its expressions to be parsed in different ways, a property of notations that has been discussed in the literature as 'multiple readability.'[92]

4.2.6 Extendability

When praising notation systems of the past, the fact that a system can be extended is often brought forward. For example, the Indo-Arabic numerals, originally intended to represent natural numbers, can be extended with a '−' sign to represent negative numbers and with a decimal point to represent non-integer rational numbers. In other words, it is considered to be an advantage if a notation can easily be extended to cover subject matters for which it was not designed. This feature of a notation, however, is most often discovered only after the notation has been in use, which means that it could not have played a role in the adoption of the notation in the first place. Thus, when discussing the introduction of notations we have to distinguish between features that were considered at the time of the adoption and those that emerged only afterward, as a fluke, so to speak. In the latter case, a notation can open up unforeseen conceptual possibilities and thus play a role in the further advancement of a science, a philosophical issue we shall return to later, in Section 5.2.3.

When weighing the importance of the extendability of a notation, it is again crucial to consider the tasks that one wants to employ the notation for. For example, the fact that in Leibniz's notation for derivatives the variable of differentiation is given explicitly, for example, in $\frac{dx}{dt}$, allows one to extend its range of application to cases where it is different from t. Such an extension is not possible in Newton's original notation, $\dot{x}$, where the variable of differentiation is left implicit. From a theoretical point of view, this speaks in favor of Leibniz's notation. However, if such an extension is not needed, because all one is interested in are derivatives of a function with respect to time (as is often the case in physics), then Newton's notation is more concise and therefore preferable. As other examples before, this brief discussion shows how important it is to relativize the assessment of notational systems to specific tasks.

4.3 Ease of Manipulations and Computational Efficiency

4.3.1 Ease of Manipulations

Since the manipulation of expressions is an integral component of mathematical notations, they are often designed in such a way to make it easier to perform some specific manipulations. As we have seen, the grouping of characters into complex symbols facilitates the parsing of expressions, but also

[92] Schlimm and Waszek (2020).

their manipulations, as complex symbols can be treated as a single unit. In the following, some examples will be discussed to show how the desire to facilitate manipulations can affect notational design.

Examples from symbolic logic are particularly illustrative, because here the inference rules (i.e., the rules for manipulating expressions) are often formulated explicitly. Some aspects of Frege's *Begriffsschrift* notation for logic can indeed be explained by his aim of analyzing logical reasoning into simple rules. Thus, instead of directly representing the logical connectives for 'and' and 'or,' which are frequent in natural languages, he chose negation and implication as primitives for his system, because then one could use just a single inference rule, namely *modus ponens* (together with substitution). Note, that this is a decision on how to carve up the subject matter, and thus which primitives to use for the notation, but does not yet determine the particular mapping between the primitives to characters and their arrangements. However, Frege's non-linear representation of the conditional makes inferences by modus ponens particularly perspicuous, as it simply amounts to cutting off the lower branch of a formula:

	Premises		Conclusion
Contemporary notation:	A	$A \rightarrow B$	B
Frege's *Begriffsschrift*:	—— A	——┬—— B └—— A	—— B

The fact that the main connective is always the leftmost one in a *Begriffsschrift* formula, whereas its location is not fixed in a contemporary formula (i.e., it is not always in the middle of the expression as the simple example shown here might suggest), makes the difference between these two notations even more striking in the case of more complex formulas.

Among the popular contemporary notations in logic are adaptations of Gentzen's *Natural Deduction* and *Sequent Calculus*.[93] Here, there are at least two inference rules (introduction and elimination) for each connective. Again, this approach depends on how to carve up the subject matter of logic but does not determine other aspects of notational design. The main notational difference between these two logical calculi concerns how the assumptions in a proof are arranged: In Natural Deduction they occur on top of a branch in the proof tree, and in the Sequent Calculus they are represented explicitly in every expression in which they are used. Without going more into the details, it should be intuitively clear that expressions in the Sequent Calculus are longer (because they always contain copies of the assumptions), but that this makes it

[93] Gentzen (1935).

easier to track the assumptions in complex proofs. This is a notational trade-off that results from different approaches to manipulating the logical formulas in proofs.

Some choices of notations for numbers and their operations have also been guided by the kind of manipulations that one wants to perform on them. For example, the predominant use of binary representations for numbers in digital computers can be explained by the relative ease in which arithmetical operations on binary numerals can be performed using simple logic gates that can be implemented with transistors. Indeed, the ease with which arithmetical operations can be carried out in the binary system was already pointed out by Leibniz.[94] Another example is the use of postfix (or reverse Polish notation, RPN) for some pocket calculators, because it lends itself to efficient evaluation. When evaluated from left to right, as soon as an operand is encountered, the intermediate value can be computed on the basis of previous computations, which can be implemented easily with a stack data structure. For the same reason, early computer implementations to determine logical tautologies represented formulas in a structure like the Polish notation.[95]

4.3.2 Computational Efficiency

Since there is an open-ended number of tasks that notations can be employed for, one frequently restricts the study of notations to some very specific ones that are deemed more relevant or insightful than others. We should be aware, however, that any such choice can already stack the odds against one notation over another.

To illustrate some of the complexities involved in assessing notations in relation to a specific task, let us briefly compare the addition of two numbers represented with Indo-Arabic and (non-subtractive) Roman numerals:[96]

LII + XVIII vs. 52 + 18

For the uninitiated reader, the case of Roman numerals might look daunting at first, since there are clearly more symbols to be processed and the value of the numerals might not be immediately obvious. For the addition task, however, all that needs to be done is to collect all symbols together ('LIIXVIII'), sort them by increasing order of their value ('LXVIIIII'), and simplify the occurrences of five 'I's to a 'V' ('LXVV') and the resulting occurrences of two 'V's to an 'X', which yields the final result 'LXX'. Now, to perform the corresponding

[94] Strickland and Lewis (2022, 196).

[95] Bauer (2002).

[96] In the non-subtractive Roman numerals, four is represented by 'IIII' instead of 'IV'. Throughout history, both subtractive and non-subtractive variants were used side by side.

addition with the Indo-Arabic numerals, we have to process them separately by their powers (i.e., first the units then the tens). To add '2' and '8', we have to have memorized the result (i.e., no simple moving around the symbols '2' and '8' will give us '10'). Of this result we keep the digit in the unit position and add the digit in the tens position to the two other digits in the tens position of our original problem (5 + 1 + 1). Again, the result, '7', has to be retrieved from memory and put into the tens position of the sum, yielding '70'.

This simple example shows what the addition of two numerals requires in the Indo-Arabic system: splitting up the numerals by their powers and processing them separately in a fixed order (from right to left), having memorized an addition table, and taking care of carries when the numeral that results from a single-digit addition is greater than 9. In the case of Roman numerals, less mental effort (both in long-term and working memory) is required, as more manipulations (such as collecting and sorting) can be carried out directly on the symbols: we only need to memorize the order of the symbols, and for each symbol a simplification rule (e.g., five 'I's make a 'V'). As a consequence, learning to perform additions is easier in the case of Roman numerals than it is in the case of Indo-Arabic numerals. However, once the relevant facts and algorithms have been memorized and mastered, the calculation in the Indo-Arabic system is more concise, as it involves fewer symbols, but the algorithms can be more complex, as they need to keep track of the position of the digits.[97]

To extend this line of comparative inquiry, we could now look at further arithmetical operations and other tasks, such as writing a list of numbers, extending and generalizing the systems to include negative numbers and fractions, and so on. To assess the use of notational systems 'in the wild,' we could also try to find out what tasks they are actually used for in practice and which manipulations are most frequently employed. In light of the problem of familiarity, it is imperative to avoid cherry-picking the tasks and examples that support one's favorite notation. In general, the more systematic and comprehensive an assessment is carried out, the more meaningful it is – though perhaps also less sensationalist.

5 Notations and Philosophy

Now that we have a characterization of mathematical notations in place, discussed their components and have seen how they play a role in practice, and also went over considerations regarding their design and assessment, we now

[97] For a more nuanced comparative assessment of computations with Roman and Indo-Arabic numerals, see Schlimm and Neth (2008) and Lengnink and Schlimm (2010).

turn to the relation between the study of notations and more traditional philosophical questions. Philosophers have often neglected notations because there is a sense in which they are arbitrary. After all, so the argument goes, it is difficult to imagine how arithmetic would be different if the symbol '#' had been adopted instead of '8'. Then again, if some role is attributed to notational systems, this is often in the context of claiming superiority of contemporary notations, where the exact role of the notation is often a matter of speculation rather than based on actual evidence (e.g., one can frequently read the claim that decisive mathematical advances were possible only after the Roman numerals had been replaced by the Indo-Arabic ones – despite the fact that basic computations are also possible with Roman numerals and that a place-value system was available in Mesopotamia before the Roman numerals). We have seen that notations can be motivated by and have an effect on many aspects of mathematics, so that their arbitrariness concerns only the relation to an abstract and idealized notion of mathematical truth. Once we leave the latter aside, many philosophical questions arise in relation to mathematical notations.

The discussions in the previous sections have hinted at various ways in which notations are intertwined with particular conceptualizations of their intended subject matter, and here I bring together some of these observations to discuss their relevance for ontological and epistemological issues (Section 5.1) as well as methodological ones (Section 5.2). In the former discussion we consider notations as static, in the latter as changing dynamically over time.

5.1 Notations, Ontology, and Epistemology

5.1.1 Notations Influence and Reflect Ontological Conceptions

In the earlier discussions about the relation between a notation and its intended subject matter, we have seen that choosing a notation requires the determination of the primitives of the subject matter that are to be represented. This, in turn, amounts to carving up the subject matter in a certain way. While one might be inclined to think that there is a particularly natural or intuitive way of doing so, we should be wary that this sentiment might simply originate from a strong familiarity with one particular notation. The possibility of alternative notations, each with its own specific advantages with regard to users and tasks, questions the ideal of a unique, best, and most natural representation.[98]

A quick look at different numeral systems illustrates the point just made: Our familiar Indo-Arabic place-value notation is based on a segmentation of

[98] That there isn't one single best notation for the natural numbers has not escaped some philosophers, for example, Grosholz (2007, 266) and Kripke (2023).

numbers into multiples of powers of ten, which maps reasonably well to the structure of many languages and allows for reasonably concise expressions and their manipulations; a binary representation, on the other hand, has longer expressions, so that its algorithms typically have to execute more steps, but they typically require much less memorization; common formal representations of numbers are based on an initial element and a successor function (see p. 25), which facilitates recursive definitions of arithmetical operations and proofs by induction; finally, Euclidean representations of numbers as collections of units allow for spatial arrangements according to which we can classify numbers, for example as squares and triangular numbers:

Squares: ∘∘ / ∘∘ ∘∘∘ / ∘∘∘ / ∘∘∘ . . . Triangular numbers: ∘∘ / ∘ ∘∘∘ / ∘∘ / ∘ . . .

Just as learning expressions in a foreign language that have no obvious counterpart in one's native language extends one's way of looking at and of experiencing the world,[99] learning a new notation can change one's conception of the intended subject matter. For example, due to the irregularities of many verbal numeral systems, the base-10 structure of the verbal system is not immediately apparent (e.g., 'eleven' or 'twelve' in English), and children often realize it only *after* learning the base-10 Indo-Arabic numerals. Similarly, due to the fact that for every verbal numeral system there is a largest number that it can name,[100] many people are not aware of the possibility of naming every natural number before learning the Indo-Arabic numeral system. Of course, literate adults are so familiar with their current system of numerals that it is very difficult to even imagine conceptions of numbers that are independent of the Indo-Arabic system. Historically, however, conceptions of numbers have changed, even among mathematicians. Euclid, for example, considered natural numbers to be collections of units and since an individual unit does not yet constitute a (proper) collection, he did not consider 0 or 1 to be numbers. If natural numbers are conceptualized as ordinal, or counting numbers, it makes more sense to start with 1, rather than with 0, as Dedekind did in his seminal work *Was sind und was sollen die Zahlen?* (1888). Under a cardinal conception of natural numbers, say as cardinalities of concept extensions,[101] it makes sense to consider 0 to be a number, namely the cardinality of empty concepts, such as 'elephants in my fridge' or 'round square.'

Thus, while a notational system is often based on a certain conception of the intended subject matter, learning such a system can also change a user's prior

[99] For English speakers, these include the Danish *hyggelig* and the German *Schadenfreude*.
[100] Greenberg (1978, 253).
[101] Frege (1884).

Table 3 Comparison of different notations for linear and substructural logics.

	Girard (1987)	Avron (1988)	Troelstra (1992)	Paoli (2002)
negation	$^\perp$	$\sim$	$\sim$	$\neg$
implication	$\multimap$	$\rightarrow$	$\multimap$	$\rightarrow$
conjunction	&	$\wedge$	$\sqcap$	$\wedge$
disjunction	$\oplus$	$\vee$	$\sqcup$	$\vee$
fusion/times	$\otimes$	$\circ$	$\bigstar$	$\otimes$
dual of fusion/par	⅋	$+$	$+$	$\oplus$
unit for ⅋	$\perp$	f	**0**	**0**
unit for fusion	**1**	t	**1**	**1**
top	$\top$	$\top$	$\top$	$\top$
bottom	**0**	$\perp$	$\perp$	$\perp$

conception. For this reason the arrows between notational system and subject matter in Figure 2 (p. 23) point both ways.

For the philosophy of mathematical practice, the study of notational systems can yield fruitful information about the authors', or users', conceptions of the intended subject matter. Informative examples that show how notations can reveal their authors' conceptions are given in Table 3. Similar tables are frequently given in works on linear logic and, more generally, substructural logics, which shows that the authors use their symbols deliberately.[102] Even without any understanding of the meanings of the connectives in question, the use of cognate symbols indicates which connectives the authors consider to be related. For example, Avron, Troelstra, and Paoli consider conjunction and disjunction ('$\wedge$' and '$\vee$', '$\sqcap$' and '$\sqcup$'), and top and bottom ('$\top$' and '$\perp$') to be related, whereas Girard's notation suggests a close relationship between disjunction and fusion ('$\otimes$' and '$\oplus$'), and conjunction and par ('&'and '⅋'). Additional nuances in the authors' ways of carving up the intended subject matter can be found out by taking a closer look at the notations. Notice also that while the symbols for negation and implication do not reveal any connections within the notational systems themselves, they were also chosen intentionally to mark analogies to and differences from other systems of logic.

In addition to the relations between primitives within a notational system, the choice of characters can also express a relation to other systems. This is the case, for example, in Boole's use of arithmetical symbols ('+', '×', etc.) for

[102] See, for example, Avron (1988, 161), Troelstra (1992, 21–22), Paoli (2002, 42). Thanks to Pierre Saint Germier for these references and to Sophie Marchand for bringing this topic to my attention.

his logical connectives to highlight the affinity between logic and arithmetic, which we have already seen above. Later writers, who wanted to show their indebtedness to Boole without also maintaining a strong connection between arithmetic and logic, changed their characters slightly. For example, instead of using Boole's '+' Peirce added a comma to the symbol ('+, '), while Jevons created a plus-like shape ('·|·'). Like Boole, also Dedekind used the familiar arithmetical symbols in his symbolization of the greatest common divisor and least common multiple to indicate structural commonalities between these operations.[103]

5.1.2 Notations Raise Ontological Questions

What some of the discussions of the previous examples show is that some questions about the nature of the intended subject matter originate from considerations about particular notations. For example, taking up the discussion of notational artifacts in Section 3.1.4, arithmetical operations and logical connectives, such as '+' and '$\wedge$', are typically introduced as binary, which requires the use of parentheses and the law of associativity; furthermore, a linear representation also forces an order of the arguments, which requires the commutativity law. But, is this really the most appropriate way of characterizing the subject matter? In the notation of Peirce's Existential Graphs, in contrast, logical conjunction is an n-ary operation without any particular order among its arguments. The graph 'ABC', for example, represents formulas such as those expressed by '$(A \wedge B) \wedge C$' or '$(C \wedge A) \wedge B$' in a contemporary linear notation. These examples illustrate how different notations can incorporate different assumptions about the intended subject matter. And, given the abstract nature of the subject matter, it can be difficult to identify and assess these ontological assumptions independently of any notation.

Another simple, but perplexing, example of a philosophical question that is raised by the adoption of a particular notation also comes from classical propositional logic. Here, the expressions 'A' and '$\neg\neg A$' have the same truth value. But, assuming that we take propositional logic to be about propositions, do these expressions also represent the *same* proposition? To answer this question we would need a conception of propositions that is independent of their particular representations. By looking at Frege's reflections we can see that the question is indeed a difficult one. For him, logical formulas have a truth value (their reference) and express a thought (their sense). A criterion that emerges from his writings about whether two thoughts are the same is that "a speaker

[103] See Haffner (2021, 19).

who understands both of them and assents to one must, on pain of incoherence, also be disposed to assent to the other."[104] So far, so good. But, does this settle the question about the thoughts expressed by double negation formulas? Frege himself appears to be of two minds: In Part I of his *Logical Investigations* (1918–19) he speaks of 'A' and 'the negation of the negation of *A*' as being *two* thoughts, albeit with the same truth value, but in Part II (1923–26) he writes that "'not(not B)' has the same sense as 'B'."[105]

In the absence of an alternative notation for logical negation one might wonder how the situation with double negations could be otherwise. But, in fact, there are logical notations for which the preceding question does not arise. In an early work on symbolic logic from 1847, De Morgan uses '*a*' for the contrary of '*A*', and '*A*' for the contrary of '*a*'.[106] Thus, in this notation the difference between a formula and its double negation cannot even be expressed!

A quick look at a discussion by Jevons of the advantages and disadvantages of De Morgan's notation is instructive. The practical problem of not being able to apply negation to complex formulas can be overcome by considering only normal forms in which only literals can be negated, something that Jevons did. When comparing his choice with that of MacColl, who uses a prime ('′') to indicate negation, Jevons writes:

> In one point, no doubt, his notation is very elegant, namely, in using an accent as a sign of negation. A' is the negative of A; and as this accent can be applied with the aid of brackets to terms of any degree of complexity, there may sometimes be convenience in using it. [...] but it is not often needed. In the case of single negative terms, I find experimentally that De Morgan's Italic negatives are the best. The Italic *a* is not only far more clearly distinguished from *A* than is A', but it is written with one pen-stroke less, which in the long run is a matter of importance.[107]

This quote is very instructive for the philosophy of notations, as it illustrates how a typical assessment of a notation by an experienced user does not focus on one single aspect, but weighs different aspects against each other. First of all, we notice that Jevons does not bring up any foundational considerations that are related to the intended subject matter, but only practical ones. Second, 'elegance' seems to be understood as conciseness, but is not given much weight in the assessment. The generality of the notation, namely that negation can be applied to any terms and not just individual variables, is acknowledged,

[104] Blanchette (2012, 33).
[105] Frege (1984, 389 and 399).
[106] De Morgan (1847, 55–56). An analogous notation was proposed by Ramsey, who suggested to form the negation of an expression by writing it upside-down (Ramsey 1927, 161–162).
[107] Jevons (1896, xv).

but downplayed with reference to the frequency of these applications. So, here Jevons appeals to the uses in particular tasks, but leaves it open what exactly these tasks are. His choice of notation for negation is ultimately based on his own experience with using the notation. In particular, he points out the ease of reading (i.e., distinguishing '*A*' from '*a*' is easier that distinguishing '*A*' from '*A′*') and writing. Interestingly, Jevons does not mention the additional parentheses that are required for MacColl's negation when applied to complex terms, nor the need to use a canonical form when using his own notation. To summarize in terms of the aspects of notations discussed in Section 3, it is the tasks and users that are given most weight by Jevons. That this assessment is in the end relative and ultimately a matter of personal preference is made clear by his statement immediately following the preceding quote: "The student, of course, can use A' for a whenever he finds it convenient."[108]

5.1.3 Notational Invariance and Plurality

The possibility of alternative notations, and thus also of alternative conceptualizations of a certain subject matter, has not escaped completely the attention of philosophers. And while some have seen this as an opportunity to argue for the superiority of a particular system, others have incorporated this into their philosophical methodology. As an example for the latter, Wittgenstein writes in his *Tractatus*:

> 3.342 In our notations there is indeed something arbitrary, but *this* is not arbitrary, namely that *if* we have determined anything arbitrarily, then something else *must* be the case. (This results from the *essence* of the notation.)
>
> 3.3421 A particular method of symbolizing may be unimportant, but it is always important that this is a *possible* method of symbolizing. And this happens as a rule in philosophy: The single thing proves over and over again to be unimportant, but the possibility of every single thing reveals something about the nature of the world.[109]

Here Wittgenstein claims that what really matters is what is invariant across different notations. Accordingly, if one is interested in investigating a subject matter, one should study different notations for it.

Wittgenstein's view is based on a particular understanding of what a subject matter is and on the availability of expressively equivalent notations, both assumptions which are debatable. Nevertheless, he has a point in the usefulness of studying equivalent notations, which can be illustrated by the following

---

108 Jevons (1896, xvi).

109 Wittgenstein (1922, italics in original).

simple examples. A unique way of representing rational numbers is to use irreducible fractions, that is, fractions in which the numerator and denominator do not have any integer factor greater than 1 in common. However, since this complicates the definition of arithmetical operations, rational numbers are typically represented by ordinary fractions, where different expressions end up referring to the same number, such as '1/2', '2/4', '3/6', and so on.[110] In a mathematical setting, we could use equivalence classes of such expressions to identify the rational numbers. In addition, rational numbers can also be represented by decimal expansions, such as '0.5' and '0.333 . . .,' at the cost of introducing the need for infinite expressions; this can be avoided by using some notation for repeating sequences of digits, such as '$0.\overline{3}$' for '0.333 . . . '. The length of these repeating sequences, which is primarily an artifact of this particular notational system, can then be used to classify and further study the rationals. Thus, each of these notations brings out some aspects of the rational numbers, and by understanding the relationships between them, a more comprehensive notion of rational numbers is obtained. This plurality of possible notations can also be interpreted in support of the open-endedness of mathematical concepts.[111]

The plurality of notations for a mathematical notion is also nicely illustrated by different notations used in the study of knots, which have received a considerable amount of attention as examples of the use of diagrams in mathematics.[112] Without going into the various issues raised in these discussions, I want to highlight here the fact that many of these notations are not informationally equivalent (see Section 4.2.2). However, instead of interpreting this as evidence that the notations are about different subject matters, we can also see them as rendering the same subject matter at different levels of representational granularity.[113] As Brown, who interprets this in support of mathematical platonism, puts it: "Each picks out different things. Of course, they overlap to some extent, but there are properties that one notation can describe that others cannot."[114]

Another example for the plurality of notations, even when used by a single author, are the different variants of Peirce's Existential Graphs, such as the non-linear versions shown in Figure 4 as well as linearized versions using different kinds of parentheses and brackets, such as '$A(CD(G(P(R)(Q))(N)))$',

110 A similar situation arises with decimal expansions of real numbers, where different representations '1.000 . . . ' and '0.999 . . . ' refer to the same number.

111 Waszek (2024).

112 See Brown (2008) and De Toffoli and Giardino (2014).

113 Manders (1996).

114 Brown (2008).

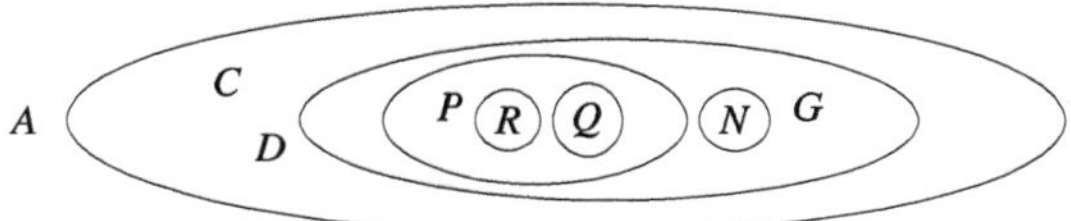

(a) Existential Graph using ovals, as described by Peirce.

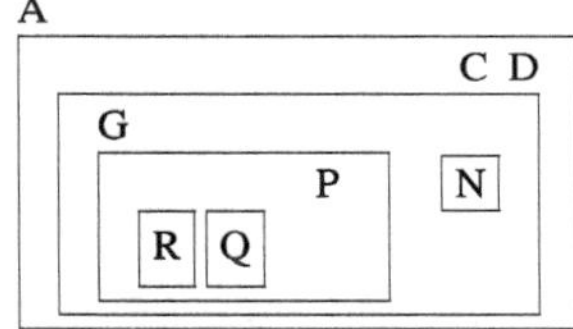

(b) Existential Graph, shown in Couturat et al. (1902, 648).

Figure 4 Non-linear variants of Peirce's Existential Graphs.

'*A*(*CD*[*G*{*P*(*R*)(*Q*)}{*N*}])', and '*A*(*CD*[*G*(*P*[*R*][*Q*])(*N*)])'. In all of these examples, the inclusion relations, which indicate the negation of an expression, are the same. In the second linear version, different kinds of parentheses are used for easier detection of matching parentheses. To reason with these expressions, one must distinguish further between cases where a subexpression is enclosed an even or an odd number of times. This information is implicit in the first two linear expressions and in Figure 4(a), but is represented explicitly in the third linear version, where the shape of the parentheses indicates odd or even inclusions, and also in Figure 4(b), where odd inclusions are written on the right side of a box. A careful study of these variants reveals a number of trade-offs between these different notational variants.

5.1.4 Notations and Norms of Reasoning

Moving away from considerations about the subject matter, the study of mathematical notations in practice can also reveal norms of reasoning that are characteristic for particular practices.[115] Through their reliance on specific representations and conventions, these might differ from generally accepted contemporary norms of mathematical rigor. Particularly influential in this regard has been Manders' analysis of reasoning in ancient Euclidean geometry.[116] While intuitive diagrammatic reasoning was criticized in the late nineteenth century for its danger of unwarranted inferences, this practice has shown to be remarkably stable. By studying the interplay between text and diagram, Manders identified two kinds of properties of Euclidean diagrams: *exact* and *co-exact properties*. The latter, such as inclusions or points of intersection,

115 See Waszek (2024) for a discussion.

116 Manders (2008).

are invariant through a range of deformations and thus not as sensitive to features of the drawing, such as exact angles and lengths. The information that Euclidean geometric practice takes from diagrams is always co-exact, which, according to Manders, is the basis for the reliability of the practice. This work has fueled a renewed interest in diagrammatic and informal reasoning in mathematics.

5.2 Notations and Methodology

5.2.1 Classifications and Notational Developments

An important part of a philosophy of notations is the classification of notational systems, because this allows for their systematic comparison and for the identification of trends in the historical development of notational systems. Such classifications, or typologies, depend on the nature of the intended subject matter, the notational elements of the systems that are used in the classification, a ranking of these elements (in the case of hierarchical typologies), and on the particular purpose of the classification itself.[117]

As an illustration for the classification of notational systems, let us consider numeral systems, which have attracted considerable scrutiny not only from historians and philosophers, but also from cognitive scientists and mathematics educators. The following typology is intended to offer a systematic overview of the ways in which the values of expressions are determined using the representation of the base and multipliers as main notational elements.[118]

Abstractly, we can represent the value n of a numeral expression in a system with *base* b as the sum of products of *multipliers* m_i (ranging between 0 and $b - 1$) with powers of the base:

$$n = (m_k \times b^k) + \cdots + (m_1 \times b^1) + (m_0 \times b^0).$$

For example, the value of the numeral '959' in the Indo-Arabic system is $(9 \times 10^2) + (5 \times 10) + (9 \times 1)$. On the basis of this analysis, we can distinguish numeral systems according to how the values of the base powers and multipliers are represented. In the typology shown in Figure 5, the powers of the base can be represented by their *position* (as in the case of Babylonian and Indo-Arabic numerals), by an *explicit symbol* (as in the case of the numerals in the Texcocan Kingsborough Codex and Chinese numerals), or by being *integrated* in the same symbols that are used to represent the multipliers (as in the case of the Roman and Greek alphabetic numerals). The representation

[117] See Widom and Schlimm (2012).

[118] Widom and Schlimm (2012), based on an earlier typology by Chrisomalis (2010).

Multiplier representation	*Base power representation*		
	Integrated	**Explicit (parsed)**	**Positional**
Cumulative	Roman	Texcocan	Babylonian
	DCCCCLVII	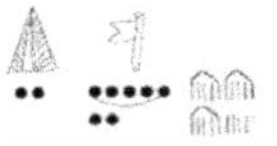	
Ciphered	Greek alphabetic	Chinese	Indo-Arabic
	ϡνθ	九百五十九	959

Figure 5 A typology for numeral systems based on the representations of the base and the multipliers.

of the multipliers can be *cumulative*, by repeating a symbol (as in the case of Roman and Babylonian numerals as well as those in the Texcocan Kingsborough Codex), or *ciphered*, by using a distinct symbol for each multiplier (as in the case of the Greek alphabetic, Chinese, and Indo-Arabic numerals). Another typology, by Zhang and Norman (1995), which is frequently referred to in the literature on mathematical cognition, uses the 'dimension' of a numeral system, namely whether the system has a base or subbase, as the single most important notational element, because the authors consider this to be most relevant for calculations.

Using such a classification of numeral systems, Chrisomalis studied the historical development of most extant systems of numerals and identified various regularities regarding the change of numerical notations over time, such as 'No ciphered system has a subbase' and 'Cumulative systems do not develop from noncumulative ancestors' (Chrisomalis, 2010, 368, 384). Thus, we see here how a classification of notational systems, together with a historical study of their changes, can lead to general insights into the development of notational systems. These, in turn, can further be studied in terms of their motivations, such as the cognitive resources they require and the tasks that they were employed for.

5.2.2 Patterns of Notational Change

Particularly frequent patterns of notational change are *grouping* and *symbolization* (or ciphering). For example, to increase the readability of a sequence of tallies, '||||||||', we can group them into smaller collections, as in '||||| |||'. In Sections 2.2.6 and 3.2 we have also seen how the grouping of Indo-Arabic digits facilitates the parsing and verbalization of numeral expressions. These groups can be perceived and treated as a single unit, thus having all the advantages of complex symbols (Section 4.2.5). If, instead of simply grouping together subexpressions, we replace them by a new character, we speak of *symbolization*. In the tally example this can be '卌' or a single character, such as 'V'. While grouping generally increases the length of expressions, symbolization decreases it – at the cost, however, of introducing a new character whose meaning has to be memorized. By repeated grouping and symbolization, notations become more and more concise, and more expressively powerful, but at the same time more cognitively demanding.

In the history of symbolic logic we can also identify certain notational trends, both with regard to the structure and the characters employed in logical formulas: The equational form and the use of arithmetical symbols introduced by Boole slowly disappeared and were retained in the twentieth century only by some logicians in the algebra of logic tradition. The dot-notation for grouping, introduced by Peano and popularized by Russell and Whitehead's *Principia Mathematica* (1910), was replaced in subsequent decades by the use of parentheses. Following Heyting's introduction of the symbol '¬' for negation (to distinguish syntactically between classical and intuitionistic negation),[119] this slowly replaced the earlier '~', just as '∧' seems to have replaced Hilbert's '&' for conjunction, although all of these symbols are still in use today. As of today, identifying further trends, possibly in terms of traditions and schools, and addressing questions regarding their motivations remains an open and underexplored area of research.[120]

5.2.3 Blocking Off and Opening Up Conceptual Possibilities

In her groundbreaking study of the development of notations in chemistry, Klein convincingly argued that "paper tools, like laboratory tools, are resources [...] whose application generates new goals, objects, inscriptions, and concepts linked to them."[121] This insight has been carried over also to mathematics by Grosholz, who wrote that "the study of mathematical rationality cannot dispense with the study of representations."[122] In short, any study of methodology in science and mathematics should include some discussion of the role of notations.

We have seen in the example of De Morgan's symbolism for negation that his notation does not allow one to express the double negation of a formula. In other words, the equivalence of a formula and its double negation is baked into the notation, and, as a consequence, questions regarding the difference between 'A' and '$\neg\neg A$' simply do not arise for users of De Morgan's notation. Systems of intuitionistic logic, where the meaning of negation is different from

119 Heyting (1930, 43).

120 As examples of such work, see Bellucci et al. (2018) and Schlimm (2018).

121 Klein (2002, 3).

122 Grosholz (2007, xiii).

Table 4 Representations of powers of an unknown quantity in the history of algebra.

Contemporary:	x	x^2	x^3	x^4	*mne.*	*num.*	*mod.*
Diophantus:	ς	Δ^Y	K^Y	$\Delta^Y\Delta$	✓		
Xylander, 1575:	N	Q	C		✓		
Bombelli, 1572:	$\underset{\smile}{1}$	$\underset{\smile}{2}$	$\underset{\smile}{3}$			✓	
Stevin, 1594:	①	②	③			✓	
Vieta, 1591:	A	Aq	Ac	Aqq	✓		✓
Harriot, 1631:	a	aa	aaa				✓
Hérigone, 1634:	a	$a2$	$a3$	$a4$		✓	✓
Descartes, 1637:	x	xx	x^3	x^4		✓	✓

Note: The columns on the right indicate whether the notation uses mnemonics (*mne.*) or numerals (*num.*) for the powers of the unknown and whether the powers are represented by a modification (*mod.*) of a symbol for the unknown.

that in classical logic, so that the inference from '$\neg\neg A$' to 'A' is not valid, could thus not be formulated with De Morgan's notation, but would require a different way of representing negation. Thus, a simple move toward intuitionistic logic is not available for users of De Morgan's notation. The notation blocks off this conceptual possibility.

Let us now look at some examples from algebra to illustrate how notations can open up or block off further conceptual developments. In particular, we shall focus on representations of the powers of an unknown (see Table 4).[123] Early algebraists used only a single unknown in an equation, which, in the case of the third-century Greek mathematician Diophantus, was written as 'ς'.[124] For the second and third powers of the unknown, Diophantus uses 'Δ^Y' and 'K^Y', which are derived from the first letters of the Greek words for square (δύναμις) and cube (κύβος). Thus, we notice the mnemonic origins of these symbols, but, and this is more important for our discussion, there is no direct connection between the symbols for the unknown and the value of their powers. The same is true when the work was translated into Latin, for example, by Xylander, who used 'N', 'Q', and 'C', mnemonics for the Latin *numerus*, *quadratus*, and *cubus*.[125]

[123] For an account of the emergence of these symbolic devices, see Wagner (2017, 39–58).

[124] The exact shape and origin of this symbol is disputed in the literature; see Heath (1910, 32–35). We here follow Heath's usage.

[125] Heath (1910, 38).

A change of notation with far-reaching consequences occurred when numerals began to be used for the powers of the unknown, for example, by Bombelli and Stevin. However, these had to be distinguished symbolically from ordinary numerals, since the latter were also used for the coefficients of these powers. To do so, Bombelli put the powers above a semicircle and Stevin enclosed them within a circle. Once the powers are associated with numbers, it becomes possible to express concisely relations between powers in terms of relations between numbers, such as (in modern notation) $x^2 \times x^3 = x^{(2+3)}$, as well as general laws about them, such as $x^a \times x^b = x^{(a+b)}$. In addition, this use of numerals can easily be extended further in two ways: First, we can use the notation to represent any power without having to introduce new names and symbols, and, second, we can replace the representations of whole numbers by other kinds of numbers, including zero and rational numbers. Indeed, this is what Stevin did, for example, by using ⓪ for terms that do not depend on the unknown and (1/2) for square roots of the unknown. In this case, an exponent can be interpreted as repeated multiplication, as the vanishing of the unknown, or as taking the square root. This use of numerals can be seen as an example of what Grosholz called "productive ambiguity" and which she argued is a powerful methodological principle for driving progress in mathematics and science.[126] The move away from the traditional mnemonics is also a further step away from associating the powers with a geometrical interpretation and thus a step toward a reconceptualization of the intended subject matter.

An even more decisive development in the history of algebra was the introduction of a systematic notational connection between the unknown and its powers. Vieta, in particular, while retaining the mnemonic for the powers, used 'A' for the unknown, 'Aq' for its square, and so on. Harriot, who had introduced a similar practice earlier, simply used a cumulative notation to indicate the powers: 'a', 'aa', 'aaa', and so on. Harriot's and Vieta's moves help to keep track of more than one unknown quantity in an equation, thus making it easier to extend the range of relationships that could be expressed by algebraic equations. The move is analogous to Leibniz's already-mentioned introduction of an explicit notation for the variable of differentiation, for example in $\frac{dx}{dt}$, as opposed to Newton's dot-notation ($\dot{x}$), with a single implicit variable of differentiation.

The move from 'aaa' to 'a_3' is worth pointing out because it can be observed as another general pattern in the development of various notational systems (see Section 5.2.2). For example, while an abacus was traditionally used by simply

[126] Grosholz (2007).

putting the desired number of pebbles on a line, such as '○ ○ ○', Gerbert of Aurillac introduced labeled tokens, such as '③'. Similarly, in order to shorten and generalize expressions with n parentheses, such as '))...))', the logician Herbrand used a single parenthesis with a numerical label, such as '$\overset{n}{]}$', and he also wrote '[m]' to indicate a group of m dots.[127] In this pattern of notational change, which we might call *numeralization*, cumulative arrangements of characters (which are easy to perceive for small quantities) are replaced by a single character with a numerical or variable label (which are more concise and can easily accommodate any number).

The two extensions of Diophantus' notation, first, by introducing a symbolic connection between the unknown and its powers and, second, by representing the powers by numerals, were developed independently of each other; but ultimately they were combined in the notations of Hérigone and Descartes, both of which are very similar to our contemporary notation. Further extensions of the notation, for example, by generalizing from '3' to 'n', or by exploring the use of '-3' and '$\frac{1}{3}$' instead of '3', illustrate again how the adoption of a notation can open up novel conceptual developments.

Another way in which a notation can lead to hitherto unthought-of possibilities is by allowing, as a notational artifact, a combination of primitives that is meaningless under the original interpretation. For this to happen, the operative nature of mathematical notations is essential. Notational artifacts have already been discussed in Section 3.1.4, so the reader is reminded here only of the most famous example in which the manipulation of meaningful expressions resulted in meaningless expressions that precipitated the introduction of a new mathematical notion, namely complex numbers. Once the use of negative numbers and the operation of taking roots had been adopted by early algebraists, their study of algorithms for the solution of polynomial equations led them to situations in which they had to take the root of a negative number. For example, in the 1545 edition of Cardano's *Ars Magna* we find him having to multiply the two terms 5. $\bar{p}$. R. $\bar{m}$. 15. and 5. $\bar{m}$. R. $\bar{m}$. 15. resulting in 25. m. m. 15, that is, 40. (In modern notation, the two terms are $5+\sqrt{-15}$ and $5-\sqrt{-15}$. In their product, $25 + 5\sqrt{-15} - 5\sqrt{-15} + 15$, the terms involving the factor $\sqrt{-15}$ cancel each other out, leaving a result of 40.) More generally, through the application of previously accepted rules for manipulating their expressions, mathematicians were confronted with expressions, such as 'R. $\bar{m}$. 15', for which they had no meaningful interpretation. After all, how could the multiplication of a number with itself yield a negative number? While many remained uneasy with these

[127] Goldfarb (1971, 220).

expressions, they were nevertheless used in the calculations, as long as they canceled out eventually and thus did not appear in the solution of a problem. Such expressions had been used successfully, albeit somewhat reluctantly,[128] for centuries before complex numbers were accepted as *bona fide* mathematical entities.

We should be careful of not oversimplifying the historical development of algebraic notations as leading to *better* notations. The focus of the preceding discussion was only on considerations regarding the way in which notations can implicitly suggest generalizations and further conceptual developments. However, whether these considerations should be the main factor in the evaluation of a notation is debatable, as the goodness of any notation depends on what we want to use the notation for. A more thorough discussion of the history of these notations should involve an identification of the tasks they were actually used for and a study of particular methods that were employed. The fact that notational changes, even if they appear obvious and straightforward in retrospect, take time to be implemented and that new notations are not adopted quickly, suggests that the adoption of a notation might have been based on considerations that are different from those we currently deem most important. We have also seen that the notations in question are not all expressively equivalent and should therefore be understood as ultimately referring to different intended subject matters. While the preceding examples illustrate some ways of opening up and blocking off conceptual possibilities, only a more detailed analysis can reveal whether the notations were the actual driving force behind later developments, or whether they were introduced to express conceptual advances; what I suspect to be the most common case is that notational and conceptual innovations go hand in hand.

6 Concluding Remarks

6.1 Summary

In the previous pages we have seen an outline of a philosophy of notations. First, we gave a characterization of mathematical notation systems: They consist of

> *characters* that are *systematically arranged* into *expressions*,
> which can be *manipulated* into other expressions by transformation rules.

In other words, the combination of character shapes, their structural arrangements, and operations on expressions determine a particular notational system.

[128] See, for example, the quote by Cauchy on p. 5.

The main conceptual and terminological distinctions of these components of notations were presented in Section 2.

To guide and focus the investigation of the use of notational systems in practice, six different aspects were introduced and discussed in Section 3 (see Figure 2 for an overview):

> (1) the intended subject matter, (2) verbalization, (3) users and their resources, (4) tasks and applications, (5) the material basis, and (6) the historical context.

As these aspects are heavily intertwined and any particular application can involve any of them, it is crucial for a systematic discussion of notational systems to try to deal with them separately.

Some of the key insights regarding the nature of mathematical notations are the following. While mathematical notations share many properties with systems of representations, they are not purely representational, because it is possible that some expressions in a notational system do not represent anything from the intended subject matter. This is a consequence of the operational, creative aspect of mathematical notational systems, which they share with natural and formal languages. In analogy with languages, learning a notational system transforms the users' cognition, so that notations do not merely express thoughts, but they can be constitutive for thoughts: We can think in symbols.

Considerations about practical aspects can also guide the design and comparative assessment of notational systems, as discussed in Section 4. Here, it is important to keep in mind that notational design is ultimately a matter of trade-offs and compromises. On the basis of these discussions, we turned, in Section 5, to more traditional philosophical questions regarding the epistemological, ontological, and methodological roles of notations. Here, we identified grouping, symbolization, and numeralization as general patterns of notational change. In addition, we have seen how design choices made for a particular notation can open up new conceptual possibilities as well as block off others. Thereby, the formulation of a notational system can sharpen and transform our understanding of a subject matter and, through its unanticipated and unintended consequences, it can also contribute in an essential way to the further development of the science.

6.2 On the Study of Notations

Because discussions of notations are often biased toward the most familiar notations, it is important to be aware of this difficulty. Methodologically, following the advice of Tolchinsky and Wittgenstein, the best way to attend to the problem of familiarity is to get very well acquainted with alternative notations and to look out for trade-offs that arise when studying different aspects of a notation. Due to familiarity and narrow focus, details can easily be overlooked, and plausible, but unwarranted, explanations taken for granted (e.g., the emphasis on the role of a symbol for zero and its relation to place-value systems for numbers). While it might be tempting to investigate sophisticated notations for advanced subject matters (e.g., Feynman diagrams for the interactions between subatomic particles, diagrams for quantum processes, or computer programming languages), the complexities of the subject matter and the necessary background knowledge can make it more difficult to identify what exactly are the contributions of the notation and what results from a specific conceptualization of the subject matter. In contrast, we have seen that even simple examples, such as those from arithmetic and propositional logic used throughout this Element, provide a rich and fruitful resource for philosophical reflections.

Since the present introduction to the philosophy of notations is also intended to provide a practical toolbox for philosophical inquiries about notations, here are twenty-five questions to reflect upon when studying notations. They are organized around the different aspects shown in Figure 2: (1) What are the characters, arrangements, and manipulation rules of the notation? (2) What is the nature of the relation to the intended subject matter? (3) How does the notation carve up the subject matter into primitives? (4) How are the primitives of the subject matter mapped onto the notational elements? (5) What new conceptual possibilities are opened up by the notation? (6) What conceptual possibilities are blocked off by the notation? (7) What is the relation to prior verbalizations of the subject matter? (8) How is the notation verbalized? (9) Who are the intended users of the notation? (10) How difficult is the notation to learn? (11) Which perceptual and cognitive resources are required for understanding the notation? (12) What are the main intended tasks for the notation? (13) What other tasks can it be used for? (14) What algorithms can be applied to solve the tasks? (15) How do the notational features influence the execution of these algorithms? (16) What are the complexities of these algorithms in terms of time, space, and required perceptual, cognitive, and computational resources? (17) What is the intended material basis for the notation and how does this affect the other aspects? (18) What is the complexity of producing inscriptions (writing)? (19) What are the notational traditions in play? (20) How can the notation, and similar ones, be classified into families of notations? (21) What is the historical development of the notation? (22) What pressures lead to changes in notations? (23) What factors, for example, pragmatic, cognitive, or sociological, contributed to the acceptance of notations? (24) Did the notational change follow a change in subject matter, or was it the other way around? (25) What are alternative (ideally, informationally equivalent) notations and how are the preceding questions answered for those?

6.3 Interdisciplinary Outlook

The conceptual clarification of the nature of notations and their components is a distinct part of the philosophy of notations. In addition, we have seen that the study of the design and use of notations also engages with and profits from insights from other areas of philosophy and other disciplines. This can be seen, on the one hand, from the fact that we included language, users, inscriptions, and historical context among the aspects of notations in practice, and, on the other hand, from the questions suggested at the end of the previous section. Thus, while ontological considerations are an important aspect in the philosophy of notations, the systematic study of mathematical notations is really a truly interdisciplinary enterprise. To conclude this Element, let me briefly sketch some of these connections.

In addition to the philosophy of mathematics and science, the study of notational systems, understood as specifically regimented languages, clearly bears upon the philosophy of language and linguistics. And, because of the close connection between notations and thought, a better understanding of notations can also be relevant for discussions in the philosophy of mind, in particular in regard to theories of extended mind and enculturated cognition, for example, regarding the notion of derived content.[129] Taking seriously the idea of notations as cognitive *tools*, the study of notations is also related to considerations regarding the effective visualization of information, such as the work of Tufte,[130] and the design of material artifacts, such as Norman's *The Design of Everyday Things* (2013).

The interplay between notations and cognition has been studied in psychology, cognitive science, and mathematics education. The sequence of numerals is frequently credited for contributing to the learning of arithmetic in developmental psychology, but there is a lacuna with regard to its exact role, including the differences that various systems of numerals can make. Similar points can be made in regard to learning the relation between symbols and their meanings. The spontaneous associations between shapes and sounds (e.g., zigzag shapes and 'kiki' versus curvy shapes and 'bouba') are well-established topics in cognitive science research,[131] but those between shapes and other semantic content

[129] See Vold and Schlimm (2020).
[130] See, for example, Tufte (2001).
[131] Ramachandran and Hubbard (2001).

(e.g., symmetric symbols and commutativity of the denoted relation) are still to be explored further.[132] This research, together with the impact of the structure of notations on the learning and understanding of mathematics, can have important consequences for mathematics education.[133] In Polya's influential guide to mathematical problem solving, an oft-used piece of advice is: "Introduce suitable notation."[134] For spelling out the notion of suitability invoked by Polya, it is indispensable to be familiar with the principles underlying notational design.

As concepts are abstract and intangible, their development can only be traced through their representations. Thus, the historical developments of notations can be an invaluable resource for the study of the history of ideas and practices. An intentionally crafted notation can encapsulate some of the considerations that went into its design and can inform the historian about a user's philosophical assumptions and thought processes. Notational changes are often due to some kind of pressure, which can be different in the case of individuals or in the case of more large-scale changes, and from the design choices of notations we can reason about their intended applications and uses. To avoid the dangers of familiarity and of drawing conclusions too hastily, a good understanding of the aspects and issues discussed in this Element will be helpful in the further systematic study of mathematical notations.

132 Wege et al. (2020).

133 See, for example, Lengnink and Schlimm (2010).

134 Polya (1954, 150).

References

Alexander, J. W. (1928). Topological invariants of knots and links. *Transactions of the American Mathematical Society*, 30(2):275–306.

Alexander, J. W. and Briggs, G. B. (1926). On types of knotted curves. *Annals of Mathematics*, 28(1/2):562–586.

Allwein, G. and Barwise, J., editors (1996). *Logical Reasoning with Diagrams*. Oxford University Press, Oxford.

Avron, A. (1988). The semantics and proof theory of linear logic. *Theoretical Computer Science*, 57:161–184.

Babbage, C. (1830). On notations. *Edinburgh Encyclopedia*, 15:394–399.

Bauer, F. L. (2002). From the stack principle to ALGOL. In Broy, M. and Denert, E., editors, *Software Pioneers*, pages 26–42. Springer, New York.

Bellucci, F., Moktefi, A., and Pietarinen, A.-V. (2018). *Simplex sigillum veri*: Peano, Frege, and Peirce on the primitives of logic. *History and Philosophy of Logic*, 39(1):80–95.

Blanchette, P. (2012). *Frege's Conception of Logic*. Oxford University Press, Oxford.

Boole, G. (1854). *An Investigation of the Laws of Thought, on Which Are Founded the Mathematical Theories of Logic and Probabilities*. Walton and Maberly, London.

Bos, H. J. M. (2001). *Redefining Geometrical Exactness: Descartes' Transformation of the Early Modern Concept of Construction*. Springer, New York.

Brown, J. R. (2008). *Philosophy of Mathematics: A Contemporary Introduction to the World of Proofs and Pictures*. Routledge, New York, 2nd edition.

Cajori, F. (1925). Leibniz, the master-builder of mathematical notations. *Isis*, 7(3):412–429.

Cajori, F. (1928a). *A History of Mathematical Notations*, volume I: Notations in Elementary Mathematics. Open Court Publishing Company, Chicago.

Cajori, F. (1928b). Uniformity of mathematical notations: Retrospect and prospect. In Fields, J. C., editor, *Proceedings of the International Congress of Mathematicians*, Toronto, August 11–16, 1924, volume 2, pages 924–936, University of Toronto Press, Toronto.

Cajori, F. (1929). *A History of Mathematical Notations*, volume II: Notations Mainly in Higher Mathematics. Open Court Publishing Company, Chicago.

Carnap, R. (1929). *Abriss der Logistik, mit besonderer Berücksichtigung der Relationentheorie und ihrer Anwendungen*, volume 2 of *Schriften zur wissenschaftlichen Weltauffassung*. Springer Verlag, Vienna.

Carter, J. (2010). Diagrams and proofs in analysis. *International Studies in the Philosophy of Science*, 24(1):1–24.

Carter, J. (2021). "Free rides" in mathematics. *Synthese*, 199:10475–10498.

Carter, J. (2024). *Introducing the Philosophy of Mathematical Practice*. Cambridge University Press, Cambridge, UK.

Cauchy, A. (1846). Mémoire sur les fonctions de variables imaginaires. *Comptes rendus des Séances de l'Académie des Sciences. Paris*, 23: 271–275. Reprinted in *Oeuvres Completes*, series 2, vol. 23, pp. 405–435, Gauthier-Villars, 1932.

Chase, W. G. and Simon, H. A. (1973). Perception in chess. *Cognitive Psychology*, 4:55–81.

Cheng, P. C.-H. (2020). Truth diagrams versus extant notations for propositional logic. *Journal of Logic, Language and Information*, 29(2): 121–161.

Chrisomalis, S. (2010). *Numerical Notation: A Comparative History*. Cambridge University Press, Cambridge, UK.

Chrisomalis, S. (2020). *Reckonings: Numerals, Cognition, and History*. Massachusetts Institute of Technology Press, Cambridge, MA.

Couturat, L., Ladd-Franklin, C., and Peirce, C. S. (1902). Symbolic logic. In Baldwin, J. M., editor, *Dictionary of Philosophy and Psychology*, pages 640–651. The Macmillan Company, London.

De Cruz, H. and De Smedt, J. (2010). Mathematical symbols as epistemic actions. *Synthese*, 190(1):1–17.

De Morgan, A. (1847). *Formal Logic, or The calculus of inference, necessary and probable*. Taylor and Walton, London.

De Toffoli, S. (2023). What are mathematical diagrams? *Synthese*, 200(86): 1–29.

De Toffoli, S. and Giardino, V. (2014). An inquiry into the practice of proving in low-dimensional topology. *Boston Studies in the History and the Philosophy of Science*, 308:315–336.

Dedekind, R. (1888). *Was sind und was sollen die Zahlen?* Vieweg, Braunschweig. English translation by Wooster W. Beman, revised by William Ewald, in Ewald (1996), pp. 787–833.

Dehaene, S. (1992). Varieties of numerical abilities. *Cognition*, 44:1–42.

Durham, J. W. (1992). The introduction of "Arabic" numerals in European accounting. *The Accounting Historians Journal*, 19(2):25–55.

Dutilh Novaes, C. (2012). *Formal Languages in Logic: A Philosophical and Cognitive Analysis*. Cambridge University Press, Cambridge, UK.

Dutz, J. and Schlimm, D. (2021). Babbage's guidelines for the design of mathematical notations. *Studies in History and Philosophy of Science*, 88:92–101.

Elkind, L. D. C. and Zach, R. (2023). The genealogy of '∨.' *Review of Symbolic Logic*, 16(3):862–899.

Enderton, H. B. (2001). *A Mathematical Introduction to Logic*. Harcourt Academic Press, San Diego, 2nd edition.

Ewald, W. (1996). *From Kant to Hilbert: A Source Book in Mathematics*. Clarendon Press, Oxford. Two volumes.

Foster, J. E. (1947). A number system without a zero-symbol. *Mathematics Magazine*, 21(1):39–41.

Frege, G. (1879). *Begriffsschrift. Eine der arithmetischen nachgebildete Formelsprache des reinen Denkens*. Verlag Louis Nebert, Halle a/S. English translation: *Begriffsschrift, A Formula Language, Modeled upon That for Arithmetic*, in van Heijenoort (1967), pp. 1–82.

Frege, G. (1884). *Die Grundlagen der Arithmetik*. Verlag von Wilhelm Koebner, Breslau. English translation by J. L. Austin: *The Foundations of Arithmetic*, Basil Blackwell, Oxford, 1953.

Frege, G. (1984). Logical investigations. In *Collected Papers on Mathematics, Logic, and Philosophy*, pages 351–406. Basil Blackwell, Oxford. Edited by Brian McGuinness.

Gentzen, G. (1935). Untersuchungen über das logische Schließen. *Mathematische Zeitschrift*, 39:176–210, 405–431. English translation: Investigations into logical deduction, in Szabo (1969), pages 68–131.

Girard, J.-Y. (1987). Linear logic. *Theoretical Computer Science*, 50:1–102.

Goldfarb, W., editor (1971). *Jacques Herbrand: Logical Writings*. D. Reidel Publishing Company, Dordrecht.

Goodman, N. (1968). *Languages of Art: An Approach to a Theory of Symbols*. Bobbs-Merrill, Indianapolis.

Greenberg, J. H. (1978). Generalizations about numeral systems. In Greenberg, J. H., Ferguson, C. A., and Moravcsik, E. A., editors, *Universals of Human Language*, volume 3: Word Structure, pages 249–295. Stanford University Press, Stanford, CA.

Grosholz, E. R. (2007). *Representation and Productive Ambiguity in Mathematics and the Sciences*. Oxford University Press, Oxford.

Haffner, E. (2021). The shaping of Dedekind's rigorous mathematics: What do Dedekind's drafts tell us about his ideal of rigor? *Notre Dame Journal of Formal Logic*, 62(1):5–31.

Haigh, T. and Ceruzzi, P. E. (2021). *A New History of Modern Computing*. Massachusetts Institute of Technology Press, Cambridge, MA.

Heath, T. L. (1910). *Diophantus of Alexandria: A Study in the History of Greek Algebra*. Cambridge University Press, New York, 2nd edition.

Heyting, A. (1930). Die formalen Regeln der intuitionistischen Logik. *Sitzungsberichte der Preussischen Akademie der Wissenschaften*, pages 42–56.

Hutchins, E. (1995). *Cognition in the Wild*. Massachusetts Institute of Technology Press, Cambridge, MA.

Jevons, W. S. (1896). *Studies in Deductive Logic: A Manual for Students*. Macmillan, New York, 3rd edition.

Kauffman, L. H. (2001). *Knots and Physics*. World Scientific, Singapore.

Kirsh, D. (1990). When is information explicitly represented? *The Vancouver Studies in Cognitive Science*, pages 340–365.

Kirsh, D. (2003). Implicit and explicit representation. In Nadel, L., editor, *Encyclopedia of Cognitive Science*, pages 478–481. Nature Publishing, London.

Kirsh, D. (2010). Thinking with external representations. *AI & Society*, 25: 441–454.

Klein, U. (2001). Paper tools in experimental cultures. *Studies in the History and Philosophy of Science*, 32(2):265–302.

Klein, U. (2002). *Experiments, Models, Paper Tools: Cultures of Organic Chemistry in the Nineteenth Century*. Stanford University Press, Stanford, CA.

Knobloch, E., editor (2016). *Gottfried Wilhelm Leibniz. De quadratura arithmetica circuli ellipseos et hyperbolae cujus corollarium est trigonometria sine tabulis*. Springer Spektrum, Berlin.

Krämer, S. (2003). Writing, notational iconicity, calculus: On writing as a cultural technique. *Modern Language Notes: German Issue*, 118(3):518–537.

Kripke, S. (2023). Wittgenstein, Russell, and our concept of the natural numbers. In Posy, C. and Ben-Menahem, Y., editors, *Mathematical Knowledge, Objects, and Applications: Essays in Memory of Mark Steiner*, pages 137–156. Springer, Cham.

Lakatos, I. (1976). *Proofs and Refutations*. Cambridge University Press, Cambridge, UK. Edited by John Worrall and Elie Zahar.

Landy, D., Allen, C., and Zednik, C. (2014). A perceptual account of symbolic reasoning. *Frontiers in Psychology*, 5(275):1–10.

Larkin, J. H. and Simon, H. A. (1987). Why a diagram is (sometimes) worth ten thousand words. *Cognitive Science*, 11:65–99.

Lengnink, K. and Schlimm, D. (2010). Learning and understanding numeral systems: Semantic aspects of number representations from an educational perspective. In Löwe, B. and Müller, T., editors, *Philosophy* of *Mathematics: Sociological Aspects and Mathematical Practice*, pages 235–264. College Publications, London.

Lorayne, H. (1992). *Miracle Math: How to Develop a Calculator in Your Head.* Barnes & Noble, New York.

Manders, K. (1996). Diagram contents and representational granularity. In Seligmann, J. and Westerstahl, D., editors, *Logic Language and Computation*, pages 389–404. Stanford University Press, Stanford, CA.

Manders, K. (2008). The Euclidean diagram (1995). In Mancosu, P., editor, *The Philosophy of Mathematical Practice*, pages 80–133. Oxford University Press, Oxford.

Menary, R. and Gillett, A. (2022). The tools of enculturation. *Topics in Cognitive Science*, 14:363–387.

Miller, G. A. (1956). The magical number seven, plus or minus two: Some limits on our capacity for processing information. *Psychological Review*, 63(2):81–97.

Miller, K. F., Kelly, M., and Zhou, X. (2005). Learning mathematics in China and the United States: Cross-cultural insights into the nature and course of preschool mathematical development. In Campbell, J. I. D., editor, *Handbook of Mathematical Cognition*, pages 163–178. Psychology Press, Hove, UK.

Nicod, J. (1917). A reduction in the number of the primitive propositions of logic. *Proceedings of the Cambridge Philosophical Society*, 19:32–41.

Norman, D. (2013). *The Design of Everyday Things*. Massachusetts Institute of Technology Press, Cambridge, MA, revised and expanded edition.

Nuerk, H.-C., Moeller, K., and Willmes, K. (2015). Multi-digit number processing. overview, conceptual clarifications, and language influences. In Cohen Kadosh, R. and Dowker, A., editors, *The Oxford Handbook of Numerical Cognition*, chapter 7, pages 106–139. Oxford University Press, Oxford.

Nuerk, H.-C., Wegner, U., and Willmes, K. (2001). Decade breaks in the mental number line? putting the tens and units back in different bins. *Cognition*, 82(1):B25–B33.

Palmer, S. E. (1978). Fundamental aspects of cognitive representation. In Rosch, E. and Lloyd, B., editors, *Cognition and Categorization*, pages 259–303. Lawrence Elbaum Associates, Hillsdale, NJ.

Pantsar, M. (2021). Cognitive and computational complexity: Considerations from mathematical problem solving. *Erkenntnis*, 86:961–997.

Pantsar, M. (2024). *Numerical Cognition and the Epistemology of Arithmetic.* Cambridge University Press, Cambridge, UK.

Paoli, F. (2002). *Substructural Logics: A Primer*. Springer, Dordrecht.

Peirce, C. S. (1870). On an improvement in Boole's calculus of logic. *Proceedings of the American Academy of Arts and Sciences*, 7:250–261. Reprinted in Peirce (1966), III, pp. 27–98.

Peirce, C. S. (1885). On the algebra of logic: A contribution to the philosophy of notation. *American Journal of Mathematics*, 7(2):180–196. Reprinted in Peirce (1966), III, pp. 210–249.

Peirce, C. S. (1897). The logic of relatives. *The Monist*, 7(2):161–217.

Peirce, C. S. (1960–1966). *Collected Papers*. Harvard University Press, Cambridge, MA. Four volumes. Reprint of 1931–1958, eight volumes. Edited by Charles Hartshorne and Paul Weiss.

Polya, G. (1954). *Mathematics and Plausible Reasoning*, volume 1: Induction and Analogy in Mathematics. Princeton University Press, Princeton, NJ.

Ramachandran, V. S. and Hubbard, E. M. (2001). Synaesthesia: A window into perception, thought and language. *Journal of Consciousness Studies*, 8(12):3–34.

Ramsey, F. P. (1927). Facts and propositions. *Proceedings of the Aristotelian Society*, Supplementary Volumes, vol. 7, Mind, Objectivity and Fact (1927), pp. 153–170.

Saidan, A. S., editor (1978). *The Arithmetic of Al-Uqlīdisī*. D. Reidel Publishing Company, Dordrecht.

Saxe, G. B. (1981). Body parts as numerals: A developmental analysis of numeration among the Oksapmin in Papua New Guinea. *Child Development*, 52(1):306–316.

Schlimm, D. (2013). Axioms in mathematical practice. *Philosophia Mathematica (Series III)*, 21(1):37–92.

Schlimm, D. (2018). Numbers through numerals: The constitutive role of external representations. In Bangu, S., editor, *Naturalizing Logico-Mathematical Knowledge: Approaches from Philosophy, Psychology and Cognitive Science*. Routledge, Abingdon-on-Thames, UK.

Schlimm, D. (2021). Peano on symbolization, design principles for notations, and the dot notation. *Philosophia Scientiæ*, 25(1):139–170.

Schlimm, D. (2022). Tables as powerful representational tools. In Giardino, V., Linker, S., Burns, R., Bellucci, F., Boucheix, J.-M., and Viana, P., editors, *Diagrammatic Representation and Inference. 13th International Conference, Diagrams 2022, Rome, Italy, September 14–16, 2022, Proceedings*, pages 185–201, Springer, New York.

Schlimm, D. and Neth, H. (2008). Modeling ancient and modern arithmetic practices: Addition and multiplication with Arabic and Roman numerals. In Sloutsky, V., Love, B., and McRae, K., editors, *Proceedings of the 30th*

Annual Meeting of the Cognitive Science Society, pages 2097–2102, Austin, TX. Cognitive Science Society.

Schlimm, D. and Skosnik, K. (2011). Symbols for nothing: Different symbolic roles of zero and their gradual emergence in Mesopotamia. In Cupillari, A., editor, *Proceedings of the 2010 Meeting of the Canadian Society for History and Philosophy of Mathematics, May 29–31, Montreal*, volume 23, pages 257–266.

Schlimm, D. and Waszek, D. (2020). Multiple readability in principle and practice: Existential graphs and complex symbols. *Logique & Analyse*, 251:231–260.

Sheffer, H. M. (1913). A set of five postulates for Boolean algebras, with application to logical constants. *Transactions of the American Mathematical Society*, 14(4):481–488.

Shimojima, A. (2015). *Semantic Properties of Diagrams and Their Cognitive Potentials*. CSLI Publications, Stanford, CA.

Siegmund-Schultze, R. (1991). Mathematics and ideology in fascist Germany. In Woodward, W. R. and Cohen, R. S., editors, *World Views and Scientific Discipline Formation*, pages 89–95. Kluwer Academic Publishers, Berlin.

Sigler, L. (2002). *Fibonacci's Liber Abaci. A Translation into Modern English of Leonardo Pisano's Book of Calculation*. Springer, New York.

Stamm, E. (1911). Beitrag zur Algebra der Logik. *Monatshefte für Mathematik und Physik*, 22(1):137–149.

Stenning, K. (2000). Distinctions with differences: Comparing criteria for distinguishing diagrammatic from sentential systems. In Anderson, M., Cheng, P., and Haarslev, V., editors, *Theory and Application of Diagrams*, volume 1889 of *Lecture Notes in Artificial Intelligence*, pages 132–148, Springer, Berlin.

Stenning, K. (2002). *Seeing Reason: Image and Language in Learning to Think*. Oxford University Press, Oxford.

Stjernfelt, F. (2007). *Diagrammatology: An Investigation of the Borderlines of Phenomenology, Ontology, and Semiotics*. Springer, Dordrecht.

Strickland, L. and Lewis, H. R., editors (2022). *Leibniz on Binary: The Invention of Computer Arithmetic*. Massachusetts Institute of Technology Press, Cambridge, MA.

Szabo, M. E., editor (1969). *The Collected Papers of Gerhard Gentzen*, North-Holland, Amsterdam.

Tolchinsky, L. (2003). *The Cradle of Culture and What Children Know About Writing and Numbers Before Being Taught*. Erlbaum Associates, Mahwah, NJ.

Troelstra, A. S. (1992). *Lectures on Linear Logic*. CSLI Publications, Stanford.

Tufte, E. R. (2001). *The Visual Display of Quantitative Information*. Graphics Press, Cheshire, CT, 2nd edition.

van Heijenoort, J. (1967). *From Frege to Gödel: A Source Book in Mathematical Logic, 1879–1931*. Harvard University Press, Cambridge, MA.

Venn, J. (1880). Review of Frege's *Begriffsschrift*. *Mind*, 5(18):297.

Vold, K. and Schlimm, D. (2020). Extended mathematical cognition: External representations with non-derived content. *Synthese*, 179(9):3757–3777.

Wagner, R. (2017). *Making and Breaking Mathematical Sense: Histories and Philosophies of Mathematical Practice*. Princeton University Press, Princeton.

Warde, B. (1955). The crystal goblet, or Printing should be invisible. In Jacob, H., editor, *The Crystal Goblet. Sixteen Essays on Typography*, pages 11–17. The Sylvan Press, London.

Waszek, D. (2024). Informational equivalence but computational differences? Herbert Simon on representations in scientific practice. *Minds and Machines*, 34:93–116.

Wege, T., Batchelor, S., Inglis, M., Mistry, H., and Schlimm, D. (2020). Iconicity in mathematical notation: Commutativity and symmetry. *Journal of Numerical Cognition*, 6(3):378–392.

Whitehead, A. N. and Russell, B. (1910). *Principia Mathematica*, volume 1. Cambridge University Press, Cambridge.

Widom, T. R. and Schlimm, D. (2012). Methodological reflections on typologies for numeral systems. *Science in Context*, 25(2):155–195.

Wittgenstein, L. (1922). *Tractatus Logico-Philosophicus*. Kegan Paul, Trench, Trubner & Co., London.

Zhang, J. and Norman, D. A. (1995). A representational analysis of numeration systems. *Cognition*, 57:271–295.

Acknowledgments

I gave my first presentation on the project of a general study of mathematical notations at the History and Philosophy of Logic Notations workshop in Tallinn, Estonia in 2015. Since then, I have exchanged countless ideas on these matters with many friends and colleagues, too many to mention here. But, rest assured, I am very grateful to you all. I restrict my thanks here to those who have provided direct feedback on a draft of this Element: Sorin Bangu, Moritz Bodner, Jessica Carter, Markus Pantsar, Roi Wagner, David Waszek, and two anonymous referees.

No Artificial Intelligence or Large Language Model technology was used by the author in the production of any text in this Element.

Cambridge Elements

The Philosophy of Mathematics

Penelope Rush
University of Tasmania

From the time Penny Rush completed her thesis in the philosophy of mathematics (2005), she has worked continuously on themes around the realism/anti-realism divide and the nature of mathematics. Her edited collection *The Metaphysics of Logic* (Cambridge University Press, 2014), and forthcoming essay 'Metaphysical Optimism' (*Philosophy Supplement*), highlight a particular interest in the idea of reality itself and curiosity and respect as important philosophical methodologies.

Stewart Shapiro
The Ohio State University

Stewart Shapiro is the O'Donnell Professor of Philosophy at The Ohio State University, a Distinguished Visiting Professor at the University of Connecticut, and a Professorial Fellow at the University of Oslo. His major works include *Foundations without Foundationalism* (1991), *Philosophy of Mathematics: Structure and Ontology* (1997), *Vagueness in Context* (2006), and *Varieties of Logic* (2014). He has taught courses in logic, philosophy of mathematics, metaphysics, epistemology, philosophy of religion, Jewish philosophy, social and political philosophy, and medical ethics.

About the Series

This Cambridge Elements series provides an extensive overview of the philosophy of mathematics in its many and varied forms. Distinguished authors will provide an up-to-date summary of the results of current research in their fields and give their own take on what they believe are the most significant debates influencing research, drawing original conclusions.

Cambridge Elements

The Philosophy of Mathematics

Elements in the Series

Philosophical Uses of Categoricity Arguments
Penelope Maddy and Jouko Väänänen

Number Concepts : An Interdisciplinary Inquiry
Richard Samuels and Eric Snyder

The Euclidean Programme
A. C. Paseau and Wesley Wrigley

Mathematical Rigour and Informal Proof
Fenner Stanley Tanswell

Mathematical Pluralism
Graham Priest

The Mereology of Classes
Gabriel Uzquiano

Iterative Conceptions of Set
Neil Barton

Introducing the Philosophy of Mathematical Practice
Jessica Carter

Mathematics is (mostly) Analytic
Gregory Lavers

Elements of purity
Andrew Arana

Husserl's Philosophy of Mathematical Practice
Mirja Hartimo

Mathematical Notations
Dirk Schlimm

A full series listing is available at: www.cambridge.org/EPM

For EU product safety concerns, contact us at Calle de José Abascal, 56–1°, 28003 Madrid, Spain or eugpsr@cambridge.org.

www.ingramcontent.com/pod-product-compliance
Ingram Content Group UK Ltd.
Pitfield, Milton Keynes, MK11 3LW, UK
UKHW022147080726
473066UK00010B/803

* 9 7 8 1 0 0 9 4 7 2 1 4 2 *